W0246744

JAMSETJI
TATA

JAMSETJI TATA

POWERFUL LEARNINGS
FOR CORPORATE SUCCESS

R. GOPALAKRISHNAN
HARISH BHAT

PENGUIN
BUSINESS

An imprint of Penguin Random House

PENGUIN BUSINESS

Penguin Business is an imprint of the Penguin Random House group of companies whose addresses can be found at global.penguinrandomhouse.com

Published by Penguin Random House India Pvt. Ltd
4th Floor, Capital Tower 1, MG Road,
Gurugram 122 002, Haryana, India

First published in Penguin Business by Penguin Random House India 2024

Copyright © R. Gopalakrishnan and Harish Bhat 2024

Photo credits: Tata Central Archives for inserts

All rights reserved

10 9 8

The views and opinions expressed in this book are the authors' own and the facts are as reported by them which have been verified to the extent possible, and the publishers are not in any way liable for the same.

Please note that no part of this book may be used or reproduced in any manner for the purpose of training artificial intelligence technologies or systems.

ISBN 9780670098071

Typeset in Sabon LT Std by Manipal Technologies Limited, Manipal
Printed at Replika Press Pvt. Ltd, India

This book is sold subject to the condition that it shall not, by way of trade or otherwise, be lent, resold, hired out, or otherwise circulated without the publisher's prior consent in any form of binding or cover other than that in which it is published and without a similar condition including this condition being imposed on the subsequent purchaser.

www.penguin.co.in

This book is dedicated to Bombay House in its centenary year, 2024. In the offices of this stately building, which houses the headquarters of the Tata Group, the philosophy of Jamsetji Tata has been nurtured by the leadership of the Group over many generations. Both authors have been privileged to work here.

Contents

Preface

This book is titled in the name of Jamsetji Tata, the founder of the Tata Group, widely acknowledged as the 'father of modern Indian industry'. This book, however, is not a biography of this legendary man.

There are many well-researched versions of his biography from the 1930s to the present time. This book, on the other hand, is focused on an extraordinary aspect that has not been documented yet. This aspect is about how the apparently simple business philosophy of Jamsetji Tata has been retained, renewed and reinvigorated for over a century and amongst generations of Tata leaders.

It is rare for a business to begin with a simple philosophy; much rarer to still be able to perpetuate that philosophy over generations with fidelity.

Therefore, this is an insightful book about Jamsetji's ideas, which holds powerful learnings for us, and indeed, for future generations as well. Ideas that inspired him to create the Tata Group in 1868 and plant the seeds of an institution rather than just a business or commercial enterprise—the House of Tata has thereafter withstood the test of time through diverse periods of colonialism, independence, socialism, liberalization to modern times.

Ideas that have guided the Tata Group for over 150 years now and helped it to attain and retain the moniker of the biggest and most consistently successful business institution in India for several decades.

Ideas that have inspired and provoked so many Tata leaders to extraordinary heights of human achievement.

Ideas that continue to be very relevant to every entrepreneur, leader, manager and student of business, because they are powerful and timeless.

In the pages of this book, these ideas unfold through thought-provoking essays and engaging stories, not just from the life of Jamsetji, but from the many generations that have followed.

Yet Jamsetji is the glacier from which these ideas have flowed down to create the vast river system of the Tata Group. That is why the title of this book reads *Jamsetji Tata: Powerful Learnings for Corporate Success*.

Both authors of this book (Gopal and Harish) have experienced the power of these learnings while working in the Tata Group for long stretches of their careers.

Since both are also writers at heart, this book is a sincere effort to bring these lessons to each of you.

R. Gopalakrishnan and Harish Bhat
Mumbai/Bangalore, July 2024

Introduction

Enterprise and management in India are about to move from adolescence to young adulthood. As India integrates into global trade and liberalizes the national economy, the upcoming twenty-five years may well turn out to be a defining period in shaping the future relations between business and society in the country. The practice of management needs to win the support of society; business must be perceived as a responsible contributor to the ecosystem. Only then can it play its true role in the national economy. In view of this, the principles by which Jamsetji Tata set up his House of Tata in the latter half of the nineteenth century are relevant and worthwhile to recount, albeit in the modern context.

During the 1800s and early 1900s, India produced some remarkable leaders who shaped the idea of India as a nation: Dadabhai Naoroji and Mahatma Gandhi in public life, Rabindranath Tagore and C.V. Raman as intellectuals, and Jyotiba Phule and B.R. Ambedkar as social activists. When it comes to industry and enterprise, the name of Jamsetji Nusserwanji Tata leaps out in a distinct manner.

Jamsetji Tata was born in 1839. He started his partnership firm Tata and Sons in 1868. The company, Tata Sons Ltd, was incorporated in 1917 and took over the business of Tata and Sons. Today, more than 150 years later, this business that is now broadly referred to as the Tata Group, continues to grow and flourish. In fact, Tata has been the pre-eminent business house in India for several decades, a position it continues to occupy until today.

The thought leadership of Jamsetji and his successors has stood the test of time and has proven its enduring quality through all these years of industrial and economic development in India. The options chosen by the leadership, the strategies it adopted and its string of commercial actions still bear vibrancy and relevance—and they are based on human values.

Globally, business and private entrepreneurship have come to be recognized as important engines of national economic growth. Business motivations have progressively become profit focused, shareholder oriented and wealth oriented, leading to periodic excesses. Faced with such greed and excesses, society has become suspicious of business. Entrepreneurship needs to win back the support of society and its faith in them as being responsible contributors to the ecosystem. Hence, the thought leadership put forward by Jamsetji Tata, which has stood the Tata Group in very good stead for over 150 years now, and made TATA a consistently trusted and admired name, is particularly relevant in today's world.

The chapters in this book contain narratives and lessons on this very topic, assembled under ten P's, as follows:

1. Philosophy . . .   backdrop
2. Purpose . . .   community
3. Progress . . .   strategy
4. People . . .   talent
5. Pioneering . . .   risk-taking
6. Persistence . . .   determination and advocacy
7. Principles . . .   governance
8. Profit . . .   responsibility
9. Perspectives . . .   a chat among four generations
10. Postscript . . .   afterthoughts

Barring the first and last two chapters (which are only essays, with no stories), each chapter contains a lead essay, accompanied by three stories which exemplify the theme of that chapter. The three stories have been drawn from the Tata Group's (i) early days (ii) middle period and (iii) contemporary period—illustrating how each theme has carried through generations.

We recognize that these Ps can apply to many entrepreneurs, both in India and elsewhere. It is the authors' view that the simultaneous emergence of all the Ps in an entity is rare. In biology and botany, such a simultaneous occurrence of qualities is called 'the emergence principle'.

Perhaps it is this emergence principle that has made it possible for the Tatas as a group to stay at the top of the list of India's business houses for so many years. The first survey of the top Indian business houses was published by the colonial government in 1939. Thereafter, when the Monopolies Act was contemplated in 1969, a list of the top business houses was published. Nowadays, such data is routinely published by stock market commentators and economic papers. The Tata Group has managed to top these lists for almost a century, a rare phenomenon in the annals of business. As is well known, the list of top business houses in India, and indeed throughout the world, keeps getting renewed—so much so that the average life of Fortune 500 companies is reported to be declining all the time.

In this context, the life of Jamsetji, his business approaches, the authentic preservation of his core principles over almost two centuries . . . are all reasons to study him.

Just as anthropologists try to figure out the secret sauce—which they call by names like *harahachibu* and *ikigai*, which mean 'controlled eating' and 'reason to live', respectively—that helps certain communities to live healthy and long, maybe our small contribution can trigger an interest in an 'Ayurvedic formula' for creating and nurturing sustainable, humane and enlightened companies!

1

Philosophy

Upon seeing the title of our new book, the reader would legitimately wonder why there is yet another book on the founder of the Tata Group. The life of the founder, Jamsetji, as well as the history of the enterprise have both been subjects of many scholarly and journalistic works. So we owe the reader an explanation for yet another book.

In essence, this is not a biography of Jamsetji Tata. It is about how he managed to integrate into one whole his philosophy, his principles, his quality of persistence and his eye for what brought profits.

Biographies of Jamsetji Tata

A new edition of a biography of Jamsetji Tata was published by Rupa India for private circulation as recently as 2015. The original biography was authoritatively chronicled as early as 1925 by Frank Harris.[1] More recently, the tireless writer, the late Russi M. Lala, published his book on the man titled *For the Love of India*.[2] There have been several articles on Jamsetji's life and the impact he left on Indian enterprise during his lifetime.

Enterprise

The history of Tata Enterprises has also been much written about. Russi M. Lala, who worked with the Tata Trusts for several years, authored an enduring book on this titled *The Creation of Wealth*.[3] Several non-Tata authors too have written about the history of Tata Enterprises. Among these are the more recent books by Shashank Shah,[4] Girish Kuber[5] and Peter Casey.[6] Indeed, one of the authors (Harish Bhat) of this book has also written about the philosophies of the Tata businesses in the form of fascinating anecdotes and stories in his two best-selling books.[7]

What new information might have been unearthed by the authors to warrant yet another book, that too on a founder of a business enterprise who lived about a century and a half ago? What we have done is marshal the existing facts on him, some not so well-known, and have analysed them to explore new perspectives on (i) how Jamsetji created a long-lasting, multi-generational enterprise and (ii) how his successors and he institutionalized these values multi-generationally in the organization.

There were certain triggers that impelled the authors to consider writing this book. Though we have used available facts, we have woven them into a different weft and warp from what has been employed before.

We believe that our book will present an entirely different montage of facts and about Jamsetji Tata and the Tata Enterprises.

What Triggered Our Endeavour

Our first inspiration was a book by Rajmohan Gandhi titled *Why Gandhi Still Matters* (Aleph, 2017). We found it to be an elegant account of what Gandhiji stood for, and the anecdotes in the book illustrate how Gandhiji practised the principles for which he stood.

The second was a speech by the noted historian Dr Ramachandra Guha delivered to top leaders of the Tata Group at an internal event in 2015.

The third was a piece of research undertaken between 2017 and 2019 by one of the authors (Gopal) with five faculty members of Bhavan's SP Jain Institute of Management and Research in Mumbai.

The fourth trigger came from our reflections on the seemingly opposite polarities of enlightenment and capitalism. Can they coexist? There is much scepticism in the broader society about their compatibility. Could the practice of capitalism ever be benign and enlightened, not just during the life of one founder but for several generations after his passing on?

The speech by Ramachandra Guha was delivered on 29 July 2015 at the Jamshed Bhabha Auditorium at the National Centre for Performing Arts (NCPA) in Mumbai. This date is celebrated every year—physically in Mumbai and virtually in the rest of the country, as also in Tatas' European, American, Australian, Asian and African centres—by the leaders of the Tata Group to reaffirm the group's commitment to business excellence and ethics. This date of 29 July happens to be J.R.D. Tata's birth anniversary. He was born in 1904, exactly 120 years ago.

J.R.D. Tata was a paragon of perfection who strove for 'excellence with ethics' in the relentless manner in which he conducted the affairs of the Tata business enterprises for over fifty years.

Guha spoke on history, a subject he knows a lot about. He spoke about who the greatest among Indians through the twentieth century were, who fundamentally shaped the idea of the India we recognize today. In the field of politics, he ranked Mahatma Gandhi at the top. In the field of literature, he mentioned Rabindranath Tagore. With reference to social impact in India, he mentioned Dr B.R. Ambedkar, and in the realm of spirituality, Swami Vivekananda. So far, no surprises.

He then dwelt on the field of industry and enterprise. In his opinion, Jamsetji Tata would count as the greatest Indian of the nineteenth century. The Tata leaders who were present were, of course, delighted to hear this. Guha went on to highlight the significant contributions of not only the founder, Jamsetji Tata, but also his successors, notably J.R.D. Tata.

There was a second trigger. Between 2017 and 2019, one of the authors (Gopal) was involved with a piece of management research conducted with five academics of Bhavan's SP Jain Institute of Management and Research (SPJIMR). In essence, the research was about identifying the green shoots from which one could reasonably predict, even if not accurately, the emerging 'business institutions' and the 'shapers' who were chiselling such enterprises.

Well-established and well-known Indian business institutions are known to be thriving and growing well after their founders have passed away: for example, the

Tata, Godrej, Bajaj and Birla companies, to name just a few. The research was to identify younger companies of about fifty years or so, which met six subjective criteria:

- The firm should have been either founded after the 1970s or should have bloomed after that, just when liberalization was around the corner.
- The shaper must be alive to be interviewed.
- The company is not controversial in the matter of its ethics, though it may not be perfect.
- It must be a public and listed company with transparent data available.
- It must be perceived as renewing, growing and relevant to the future.
- It must be seen as sustainable, honest and enlightened.

Through desk research, interviews and due diligence, the researchers aimed to hypothesize what mindset and actions characterized the leadership behaviours within these companies. The researchers wanted to identify how those mindsets, behaviours and actions had been institutionalized to give these attributes a good chance of surviving the founding leader. Naturally, this involved a lot of professional judgement—listening, analysis, reflection and discussion within the research team.

Six companies agreed to participate in the research. Six elegant, readable books were published. The companies were L&T (bloomed after 1999), Tata Consultancy Services (bloomed after 1980), HDFC group (founded around 1985), Marico (founded around 1985), Biocon (founded around 1982) and Kotak Bank (founded around

1990). The six books were aimed squarely at practitioners of management.[8]

.Another trigger was the authors' reflections on the continuing and increasing clash between capitalism and community. Each morning, the world is assaulted with news of companies that have failed financially from having taken risks beyond their prudent capacity, or of leaders who ran their company to the ground because of their personal ego and greed, or of companies which destroyed the environment in their relentless pursuit of profits, not to forget scam entrepreneurs who marketed their stories to investors more effectively than the proverbial used-car salesman. Several surveys suggest that the trust of society and community in business is at a nadir.

So, is the concept of an enlightened capitalist an oxymoron?

We were enthused and educated by a fine book authored by University of Southern California academic James O'Toole.[9] Among us, Gopal had prior knowledge of the author's erudition, having spent some quality time with O'Toole around 1997. James had conducted a fine seminar at Goa under the auspices of the Aspen Institute and the Confederation of Indian Industry (CII). In his book, James wrote mostly about the pioneer-founders of Anglo-American companies—for example, JC Penney, William Hesketh Lever, Milton Hershey and Robert Wood Johnson of J & J (who is thought by O'Toole to have coined the term 'corporate social responsibility'). His broad conclusion was that there have been several enlightened capitalists, some of whom he has written about in the book. However, his observation was that 'in only a handful did the founder's virtuous practices survive through as many as two successions in leadership'.

To paraphrase the findings of the book in our words, the enlightened capitalist can create a virtuous company, but it is rare that that virtuous philosophy is institutionalized. The challenge is to first establish a company with enlightened principles and, second, to institutionalize those principles to survive several generations of leadership changes. That is a tall order. Of course, O'Toole acknowledged that since his remit was restricted to Anglo-American companies, European and Asian companies were left out. He acknowledged that their situation may be different.

Traditional Wisdom and Vedanta

Readers may have seen a Hollywood film, *Other People's Money*, released in 1991. The story is about a takeover bid on a long-running wire manufacturing company by an investment firm. Larry Garfield from the investment company, played by Danny DeVito, is a snarling, jeering, money-in-the-eyes character. He is pitted against Andrew Jorgensen, chairman of New England Wires, played by the elegant Cary Grant. Towards the end of the film, there is an instructive and inspiring pitch by the two men at a shareholders' meeting presenting their arguments for and against the takeover. Chairman Andrew Jorgensen, arguing against the takeover, emotionally states, 'Here we build things. We don't destroy them. Here, we care about more than the price of our stock! Here, we care about people.' The film makes a point about the opposite polarities of capitalism—shareholder versus stakeholder.

What do Indian tradition and wisdom have to say in these matters? Summarizing the essence of Vedanta, as can be applied to enterprise, there are four principles a leader must always bear in mind to do business: (i) self-awareness, (ii) protection of the resources that enable one to do business, (iii) service to others rather than service to oneself and (iv) conduct of one's business with compassion.

Simple, is it not? But how can one follow this simple adage? We think our book may illustrate an approach—citing the ways of Jamsetji and his successors.

Why This Book

It occurred to the authors that Jamsetji Nusserwanji Tata might be a noteworthy example of someone who established a company with enlightened principles and also institutionalized the principles for several generations. We agreed that we should share with a wider audience the fruits of our research and the way we arrived at our views. Hence this book, which we believe espouses a distinctive point of view.

From multiple sources, the authors have concluded that Jamsetji Tata could be counted among the greatest Indians of the twentieth century, that he was undoubtedly the shaper of a venerable and long-lasting business institution in India and that his values and business virtues have survived through more than half a dozen successors over a century and a half.

The questions in our mind were many:

• What is the role of enterprise in a society?

- What was Jamsetji's secret sauce for creating a sustainable, honest, enlightened enterprise?
- How was his philosophy encapsulated in that secret sauce?
- How did his virtues get institutionalized over such a long period of time?

These questions, and many allied ones, defined the purpose of the book, which was to explore what Jamsetji Tata (and his successors) did not only to impart to their business a strong set of values but also to institutionalize these values to endure for several generations after him.

Mental Model

We needed a mental model with which to understand, (i) what constitutes a philosophy for an enterprise, (ii) how that philosophy is practised and transmitted and (iii) how it is perpetuated for a long period of time.

In doing this, we felt inspired by what we understood of how great ideas and philosophies have developed and spread in the world. Religion and new streams of thought over the centuries . . . they all suggested a model to us. We are not referring here to what happened at the point in time when a particular philosophy took birth, but rather, a mental model of how this philosophy spread and perpetuated for a very long period of time thereafter.

Think of a river like the Ganga or the Cauvery. It starts as a trickle at Gangotri or Tala Cauvery. The trickle is elegant and simple to behold, it appears easy to comprehend. That represents the core philosophy.

Gradually, as the river flows, following the natural contours of the terrain it encounters, it becomes wide and also develops undercurrents. The width and undercurrents make such a river more daunting to navigate. It does not appear simple and elegant any more. Think of the Ganga at Allahabad (now Prayagraj) or the Cauvery at Mysore Brindavan. They represent the icons and narratives that shaped the landscape through which the rivers flow.

In its final stretches, the rivers splinter into several vigorous streams and rivulets, forming a complex delta region as they bound forth to meet the ocean. Think of the Sunderbans or the Thanjavur delta. Those represent the rituals and rites of passage that the firm adopts as it rushes to its moment of chosen fulfilment.

The metaphor of the river has provided us with a four-stage mental model consisting of Philosophy, Icons, Narratives and Rituals (PIRN).

From the Gangotri of Jamsetji Tata's elegant and simple philosophy, flowing within banks structured by his iconic successors through their actions, arise the rich stories and narratives of the rituals and rites of passage that perpetuate the philosophy. The cognoscenti call this culture.

Philosophy

It is possible to interpret the philosophy of Jamsetji Tata as being derived from the Zoroastrian precept '*Humata-Hukhta-Hvarshta*', which means good thoughts, good words, good deeds.

Jamsetji was a man known to dislike public speaking. In a rare speech in 1895 before the chief commissioner of the Central Provinces, he said, 'We do not claim to be more unselfish, more generous or more philanthropic than other people. But, we think, we started on sound and straightforward business principles, considering the interests of our shareholders as our own, and the health and welfare of our employees the sure foundation of our prosperity.'

Jamsetji believed in what he practised; for a free enterprise, the community is not just another stakeholder but is, in fact, the very purpose of its existence.

Jamsetji perhaps devised the business principles he did because he recognized that he had been favoured by providence. Such a realization inculcates humility in one. In 1896, Jamsetji began a letter to the Bombay governor, Lord Reay, saying:

> Being blessed by the mercy of Providence with more than a fair share of the world's goods and persuaded that I owe much of my success in life to an unusual combination of favorable circumstances, I have felt it incumbent on myself to provide a continuous atmosphere of such circumstances for my less fortunate countrymen . . .

Several decades later, around 1969, J.R.D. Tata was addressing a gathering in Madras when he was asked how he could institutionalize social responsibility after his time. To his credit, J.R.D. Tata said he felt a valid doubt had been raised. Upon his return to Bombay, he moved a resolution at the shareholders' meetings of all his listed companies to amend their articles of association to include a clause to the effect that a key responsibility of the company was to the community, apart from responsibilities to its shareholders and other stakeholders. This was long before the '2 per cent of net profits' corporate social responsibility spend was written into the Companies' Act!

In our contemporary times Ratan Tata emphasized the same point to employees and shareholders when he said, 'Some foreign investors accuse us of being unfair to shareholders by using resources for community development . . . (It) is money that's uplifting and improving the quality of life of people in the rural areas where we operate and work . . . we owe them that . . .'

How marvellous that the philosophy outlined by Jamsetji got embedded in and perpetuated over five or six distinct chapters of leadership over a century and more! The unique aspect of Tata Group is this—Jamsetji's philosophy has got embedded as a business philosophy over several generations at the Group.

Icons: Men of Ability

Jamsetji surrounded himself with men of ability to execute his daring ideas. He was ably assisted by his contemporary, Bezonji Mehta, who lived up to 1927. When Jamsetji wanted the best global steel professionals to set up Tata Steel, he went to the US to persuade Charles Page Perin to come to India and advise him. To establish the Indian Institute of Science at Bangalore, he had the assistance of Burjorji Padshah, a brilliant and very committed adviser. During his time, J.R.D. Tata too surrounded himself with men of rare entrepreneurship and ability, like Sumant Moolgaokar, Darbari Seth, Nani Palkhivala, Russi Modi and Faqir Chand Kohli. These leaders are venerated and their accomplishments are annually remembered at the companies that they most influenced, such as Tata Motors, Tata Chemicals, Tata Steel and Tata Consultancy Services. These icons deeply believed in and nurtured the philosophy that had been articulated by Jamsetji Tata.

Narratives

The historical stories of the Tata Group, captured in the rich and elegant narratives of Russi Lala and Harish Bhat, adduce evidence to the breadth and undercurrents of the 'river' that emanated from the Gangotri of Jamsetji Tata's philosophy. Any visitor to the Tata Archives housed at Pune and Jamshedpur will see mini-museums consisting of artefacts, letters, certificates and photographs. These reflect the thoughts, words and actions of not only Jamsetji Tata, but also those of his successors, and, very significantly, those of some of the non-Tata family top, legendary leaders like Russi Mody, Sumant Moolgaokar, Darbari Seth and Nani Palkhivala. These narratives bring Jamsetji Tata's philosophy to life and are passed on with pride from generation to generation, much like religious epics and folklore. They are simple to understand, and, like all great stories, they touch both head and heart.

Rituals

When the wide and deep river containing its philosophy and narratives is ready to meet the big ocean, it is atomized into many streams, as happens in the formation of a delta.

There are several Tata rituals practised by the many Tata companies as a matter of course. New entrants to these companies participate in many of these rituals, which create a strong impact on their minds about the culture of the group. By way of illustration, here are a few 'rituals', or rites of passage:

1. Every employee is provided a copy of or has access to the books by Russi Lala on the Tata Group, especially his seminal title *The Creation of Wealth*.
2. Every Tata company signs a formal BEBPA—Brand Equity and Brand Promotion Agreement—with the parent company Tata Sons, committing to uphold the valuable Tata brand and to promote it to the best of the company's capability. Every employee signs a personal code of conduct in his or her capacity as an employee.
3. Most course participants at Pune's Tata Management Training Centre get a guided tour of the Tata Central Archives next door to it. Likewise, at the Tata Steel Training Centre at Jamshedpur too.
4. Employees are encouraged to visit, as and when possible, the Tata Experience Centre (TXC) located in Bombay House, the headquarters of the Tata Group. The TXC evokes the rich heritage of the group through a series of carefully curated exhibits and films.
5. In some of the larger units, like the Bombay House headquarters, Tata Motors, Tata Steel, Tata Power, Tata Consumer Products and Tata Consultancy Services, statues or paintings of Jamsetji Tata, J.R.D.

Tata, and some other leaders are put up prominently, in many cases at the entrance or foyer of the building, and also in Conference Rooms. They are ceremoniously garlanded on special occasions every year, and the memories of these stalwarts are evoked during these special ceremonies.

6. Every year, two commemorative and celebratory events are observed in each of the several hundred units and factories of the group, from the Bhivpuri Hydroelectric Station to the TCS office in Sweden to the Tata Steel office in the Netherlands. The first is on 3 March, the birth anniversary of the founder Jamsetji Tata. The second is on 29 July, the birth anniversary of the longest-serving chairman, J.R.D. Tata.

7. Every employee participates in an annual event in celebration of business excellence and the Tata principles of ethical conduct of business.

In sum, our mental model of PIRN, like the river, reaches out to almost every employee of the one million plus strong force that works in Tata Enterprises. This is at the core of how Jamsetji Tata's founding principles have been institutionalized over the generations.

The Approach in Our Book

We have organized our book into ten chapters that illustrate the Gangotri of Jamsetji's philosophy, through what we have called the P's. Barring the first and last two chapters, each chapter is supported by:

1. an essay to elucidate what the P it elaborates on means.
2. examples from the history of the Tata Group over the years. The idea is not only to illustrate the P under discussion but also to demonstrate the consistency with which that P has been perpetuated over many generations of leaders.

Societal Need for Enterprise

For seventy-five years, Indian policymakers have grappled with what role to assign to private industry in national economic development. India need not be socialist or capitalist; India needs sustainable, honest, enlightened (SHE) enterprises, because only SHE enterprises can create resources for investment in public health, education, culture, skill development and job creation. Enterprise leads to People Enhancement in society, and, together, Enterprise and People Enhancement lead to Citizen Ecstasy. It is to the credit of Jamsetji that he had the foresight to figure this out and acted on it, though he did not use the words that we are using today.

SHE stands for the three concurrent characteristics of enterprise—sustainability, honesty and a state of enlightenment. A sustainable enterprise means it cares for the resources that enable it to do business; an honest one means it conducts its business truthfully, sincerely, and with integrity; and an enlightened enterprise means it envisions the community as the very reason for it to do business. SHE is truly a high benchmark, worthy of enterprises striving for, doggedly and continuously: even though one may never reach the ideal. The 'feminization' of enterprise through the acronym SHE has the added benefit of imparting humanism to profit-making.

Through two seminal books, management writer Alfred Chandler argued that corporate success is due to efficient organizational structure and scale (*The Visible Hand* and *Scale and Scope*). Perhaps Chandler ignored the 'softer side' of enterprise—philosophy, culture and transmission of the values of the organization. The role of these soft aspects is the theme that we wish to explore.

In the spring of 1987, in the early days of television reporting in India, journalist Rajiv Mehrotra interviewed the legendary J.R.D. Tata. In one part of the interview, Rajiv asks whether the Tata Group is socialist or capitalist. J.R.D. responded to say that the Tatas could well be considered as 'socialist capitalist', because those seemingly contradictory 'isms' define the philosophy of the Tatas.

A Conundrum

The media reports every day and with increasing frequency the scandals caused by Icarus-like enterprises which fly too close to the sun. Surveys suggest that public trust in companies is at a low nowadays.

Is this state inevitable?

In our individual public lectures at educational institutions, we sometimes request the attendees to answer two questions with a simple show of hands. First, are sustainable, honest, enlightened (SHE) enterprises *essential* for social and economic good? The overwhelming majority answers 'yes' to the question. Second, can the expressions 'sustainable, honest, enlightened' coexist with 'enterprise'?

Less than half of the audience says 'yes' to this. Here lies a contradiction, which our future business leaders must unravel.

Our experience suggests that the aim of management education, regulations and public policy must be to nurture corporations where both SHE and enterprise can coexist. Many would agree that the SHE enterprise (note that there is no 'perfect' SHE enterprise) is *essential* for society. From time immemorial, taxes paid by merchants, along with land revenues, paid for the palace and public services. Reading the Sangam-era classic *Silapathikaram*, one learns of the high contributions and status of merchants in the ancient city of Poompuhar in Tamil Nadu.

Taxes through trade, industry and companies are an essential public good. Without generous and honest tax revenues, society will get less benefits in the form of education, culture, health and other social goods. In *The Enlightened Capitalists*, University of Southern California academic James O'Toole affirms, 'Since there could be no human progress without commerce and trade, business-like activities were initial steps towards the creation of early societies.'

The sub-title of James O'Toole's book says 'Cautionary Tales of Business Pioneers Who *Tried* to Do Well by Doing Good' (italics ours). 'Tried' suggests that indeed there were pioneers who established enterprises based on values or principles during their lifetime. However, those enterprises could not sustain the founders' values after a couple of generations. Maybe, like radioactivity, the starting energy of SHE decays through its half-life. The narratives in the O'Toole book are mostly about Anglo-American companies like JC Penney, Hershey Chocolates, Johnson & Johnson, Levi Strauss and Unilever.

Let's take the case of Hershey (we have sourced the material here from making our own inquiries, bolstered by the commentary provided by James O'Toole). Milton Hershey (1857–1945) set up a truly SHE company. Hershey may be considered as having done for chocolate what Lever did for soap. He knew no life beyond his work with milk, sugar and cocoa. Soon after he began his venture, he bought a large farmland and set up a modern, air-conditioned factory on a site in Pennsylvania. He hired architects, landscape designers and engineers. He set up a model town, much like the Jamshedpur we Indians know.

What occupied his heart was the Hershey Industrial School that he set up in 1915. It offered twelve years of free foster care, clothing, education and vocational training. In fact, he was so enlightened that he transferred the majority of his shareholding in the manufacturing company to a Trust benefiting the school. He sought no publicity for this charity because he did not make public his setting up of the trust for eight long years. Through his life the company grew, remained highly profitable and stayed private to avoid getting acquired by bigger companies. Hershey acquired an enviable reputation for socially responsible behaviour and, believe it or not, for its sustainability efforts. For a half-century after founder Milton Hershey's death, the company retained the values and principles espoused by him.

Around 2002, the first outsider was appointed to run Hershey Foods. Since he saw his job as being to increase profits for the company, he closed three plants and asked employees to pay more for their health coverage. Unfortunately, the trustees also indulged in certain objectionable actions. They entertained a bid to sell the trust's 77 per cent shareholding to Wrigley, but backed off when employees and associates took to the streets. It emerged that the trustees had used a significant amount of money for a golf course and for paying fat commissions to themselves. A decade later, the trustees, unpardonably to long-time Hershey aficionados, entertained a bid from Mondelez for a takeover.

With so much money, the boardroom of the trust had become super-commercial and toxic. There was in-fighting. Milton Hershey's values and enlightened business approach were threatened.

SHE Can Coexist with Enterprise

We were particularly interested in the development and institutionalization experiences of global corporations other than the Tata Group, to put forth our idea in perspective for the reader. We were particularly interested in the Unilever narrative, partly because one of the authors, Gopal, has direct experience of working in that firm, and partly because its example shows that the original values and principles of a firm can remain intact, though updated and modernized in its expression.

While Unilever retained the basic philosophy of William Lever, albeit modified and modernized, that was not the case with other storied names written about in O'Toole's book. 'Even when virtuous practices have been implemented, they have had relatively short half-lives in most corporations . . . most executives believe that their shareholders opposed such practices,' concludes the author. Remember that his observations pertain to Anglo-American companies.

Port Sunlight counts among the earliest as a model town in Victorian England (1870s to early 1900s). William Lever advocated and practised radical ideas for his time, such as employee welfare, societal advancement and gender equality, at a time when women in Britain were busy with the suffragette movement to secure voting rights for themselves. Lever's philosophy, as recorded by John Griffiths of Manchester Metropolitan University in his doctoral thesis, was that 'the interests of employers and employees were identical'.

Of course, readers would be aware of Jamshedpur, which was set up by the Tata Group in the early twentieth century.

'The truest and highest form of enlightened self-interest requires that we pay the fullest regard to the interest and welfare of those around us, whose well-being we must bind up with our own and with whom we must share our prosperity,' wrote Lever in 1888. By the early 1900s, Lever had substantive operations all over Europe and America.

Progressively, William Lever's success enabled him to increase in boldness, even in zaniness. He was now devising and implementing his ideas by undertaking riskier and riskier investments. In the early 1900s, young King Albert invited Lever to invest in the Belgian colony of Congo. Entering into a 50:50 partnership with the government, William Lever embarked on the Congo operations. The company provided decent wages, clean housing, schools and healthcare to a population accustomed to being exploited as slaves. Lever was quite successful in his efforts.

Convinced that his business could be a force for social good, he further expressed his conviction by purchasing two impoverished islands in the Outer Hebrides in 1918. These British islands, off the west coast of Scotland, were quite remote, almost in the Arctic zone. He was passionate about setting up a model township around a fish business there. Unfortunately, due to several reasons, the venture stumbled.

At about the same time, there was a steep fall in world commodity prices, followed by deflation, which must have been difficult to anticipate. The finances of the company became greatly stretched. William Lever wrote with frankness and despondency, 'We are not entirely masters at the present moment and I am not captain of my own ship.' Lever's finances were so stretched that he had to concede control of 'his' company to a more profit-oriented accountant, D'Arcy Cooper. A few years later, Lever was merged with the Dutch Margarine Unie to form Unilever.

According to James O'Toole, 'over the years, the company somewhat drifted from away from Lever's founding values, though not entirely'. That may be one way of putting it, but in Gopal's experience, William Lever's successors adapted to the changed circumstances, not by departing from the founder's philosophy but by adapting the narratives and rituals that helped reinforce his philosophy.

From the 1980s, as the emerging global storms became a hurricane—financialization of company balance sheets, advent of inexpensive money, demand for formalized corporate governance, short-term profit orientation, debates on profit versus social purpose, do-good ideas like planet and purpose—new ideas based on Unilever's core philosophy grew, almost as a nod to the ghost of William Hesketh Lever. Under the leadership of recent leaders of the contemporary period, the company imposed on itself goals of reducing its use of water and energy, of adopting fair-trade sourcing of its raw materials and of appointing women to half of its management positions. In the resultant collision between these new trends and the financial markets' demand for quarter-over-quarter profits, there have been, and will continue to be, undercurrents of emerging developments, but the company remains undeterred in pursuing its core philosophy and approach.

'Anglo-Dutch Unilever has maintained a strong corporate culture that stresses the nurturing of community spirit among its employees. Equally it has earned a reputation for ethical behavior,' writes James O'Toole. Historian and HBS Professor Geoffrey Jones writes, 'The concept of integrity is wider than honesty. Making money was never seen as an exclusive goal within Unilever either for individuals or for the company.'

Would the script read differently in the case of a venerable Indian group like the Tatas? Is the Tata Group seen as having consistently implemented virtuous philosophies which the founder and his successors have managed to institutionalize for longer? There may be something to this inquiry. That is indeed the thread running through the rest of this book.

This book has taken us a lot of search, research and writing. We feel sure that it is worth both the effort and time it has taken us. Our goal is to bring out the story of how Tata Enterprises originated with a philosophy, which is articulated through seven Ps that are detailed in the chapters that follow; and how the Group has thereafter institutionalized this philosophy over more than 150 years through its iconic leaders, narratives and rituals.

2

Purpose

'In a free enterprise, the community is not just another stakeholder in the business, but, is, in fact, the very purpose of its existence'—a statement of Jamsetji Tata's central purpose for the Tata Group

Management literature is replete with dissertations on corporate purpose. This is a valid subject of academic enquiry and certainly merits attention from enterprise leaders. Academics have coined several epithets to describe their distinctive take on this subject of purpose—stakeholder capitalism, conscious capitalism, enlightened capitalism, responsive business and so on. One of the authors of this book (Gopal) has written about SHE capitalism. In fact, in 1987, in the early days of television in India, journalist Rajiv Mehrotra had asked J.R.D. Tata whether Tata was socialist or capitalist. 'I don't know,' replied Tata.

While the cognoscenti can discern the subtle differences between these concepts, to the practical enterprise leader they all converge to the central theme of why the corporation exists and what the reason for its being is. As Jamsetji said at the opening of the extension to Empress Mills in Nagpur on 5 April 1895:

We do not claim to be more unselfish, more generous or more philanthropic than other people. But we think we started on sound and straightforward business principles, considering the interest of shareholders as our own, and the health and welfare of our employees the sure foundation of our prosperity.

Many successful enterprises, particularly in their early stages adopted as their business purpose something that was descriptive of their products or inspiring about them. This statement of purpose was often couched in simple slogans. For Ford it was 'A car for the common man' and for Coca-Cola 'A pause that refreshes'. At General Motors it was 'A car for every purse and purpose' and at Kodak it was 'You press the button and we do the rest'. At American Telephone and Telegraphic, it was 'One policy—one system, universal service.' At IBM it was 'Think'.

Tata has retained the same community-centric purpose consistently, though its expression has changed with the times. This chapter has three examples from the Tatas. The first story is about founder Jamsetji's action of setting up a silk farm near Bangalore. What prompted an entrepreneur in 1893, when he was heavily preoccupied with manufacturing textiles and steel and producing hydroelectric power, to consider the establishment of a silk farm? It appears that he was driven by the prospects of creating jobs for his countrymen and also developing national excellence in this industry so that India could match a world-class silk-producing nation, Japan.

The second is a story that begins with Dorabji Tata, the son of the founder, who, in the 1930s, experienced cancer within his own family when his wife Lady Meherbai Tata fell victim to leukaemia. He was astonished that mankind knew so little about the scourge of cancer, and that India would be totally unprepared as cancer could become a more prominent threat to human life in the decades to follow. In the 1930s, the Dorabji Tata Trust, to which Dorabji left all his wealth, conceptualized the Radium Institute in Mumbai, which became the original inspiration for the Tata Memorial Hospital, established in 1941.

The third story is from the 1970s, when TELCO (Tata Engineering and Locomotive Company) chairman, Sumant Moolgaokar, thought about greening and making sustainable an automobile plant being set up in Pune, concurrently with its construction. He figured that no industrial plant should be polluting and without a plan to protect and save the resources of water, air and soil, bounties the plant would consume. His was a pragmatic ESG, long before the term was invented by contemporary evangelists.

Purpose and Neeyat

Setting up an enterprise without aligning with its strategic intent and impact (*neeyat*) would be akin to raising children without imparting a sense of values and character to them early on. Neeyat is not a novel idea or jargon. It has always existed, but it has caught our attention lately.

Over Gopal's fine dinner one day in Paris with the Moroccan chairman of Indo-Maroc Phosphates Company, the discussion veered to the role of business in society. The host dropped the Arabic word *neeya* in the discussion. That is when Gopal realized that the word neeyat used by Indians has its etymology in Arabic—true intent.

The relationship between neeyat and behaviour can be imagined to be similar to that between Gangotri and India, or Vedanta and Hinduism, or the Preamble to the Indian Constitution and the Constitution itself. Neeyat is pure, inspiring and uncluttered. However, it gets interpreted as it develops. Narratives, rituals, fables and versions are added with distance and time. This is why, for example, the practice of a religion often fails to accurately reflect its original philosophy.

As an example, in his book *The Colonial Constitution*, author Arghya Sengupta argues that the current functioning of the Indian Constitution may be considered by some as not being faithful to the Preamble. This does not mean that India needs a new Constitution. The author of the book makes a case for citizens to 'engage' with the Constitution.

Likewise, in corporations, strategists advise leaders to continually engage with the neeyat or purpose of the company (the reason for its very being) and to ensure that its expression is faithful to the original intent. Apart from thinking about and appreciating the concept, there are twin practical leadership challenges in pursuing it; while neeyat is essential in the early stages of an enterprise, it also requires continual renewal, enhancement and propagation within the ever-expanding institution.

Jamsetji Tata stated that his company exists because of the community. The Tatas still think so. Jamsetji was surely influenced by the Zoroastrian principles of *Huma, Hukhta* and *Hvarshta* (good thoughts, words and deeds). Consider other examples of industrialists who were more or less contemporaries of Jamsetji.

William Hesketh Lever stated that his company exists to clean the teeming millions all over the world. He diligently applied his Congregationalist principles in business. Unilever still 'cleans' people. Andrew Carnegie (Carnegie Steel) was influenced by Swedenborg's values, and Thomas Watson Sr (IBM) by Presbyterian ideas. John Cadbury was determined to improve the world around him, and was driven by his Quaker principles.

Small Companies

Well-known or large companies are not the only enterprises who should think about neeyat. Carbon-neutral and green technologies attract much commentary all over the world; much of this discourse is perceived by lay citizens as platitude, though couched in fine language. This is evidenced, to take just one example, by the behaviour of some of the oil majors, especially American ones.

On the flip side, a nascent bleat emanates from Greenland. A 2022 start-up in the Nordics recently dispatched 20 tonnes of pure Arctic ice from the natural glaciers in the Arctic to Dubai. The company's co-founder, Malik V. Rasmussen, describes the product as the purest water in the world because it is sourced from Arctic glaciers that have been in a frozen state for 1,00,000 years! Critics have attacked the company for its 'dystopia and frivolity'. The founders firmly believe in their neeyat—that their company has been brought into this world to help Greenland grow economically with a product that is natural, environment friendly and of social value. The company has also committed to becoming fully carbon neutral.

Here is another little-known but less exotic example: Kiran Deep Sandhu's recent book on Sardar Pritam Singh and how he helped to change the landscape of hilly Nepal. Singh has the reputation in that country as 'the transport king of Nepal', though he himself described his neeyat by saying, 'India is my *janmabhoomi*, and Nepal is my *karmabhoomi*.' He is credited with ushering in commercial transportation in Nepal in 1959 and played a major role in developing the logistics industry in the challenging terrain of that country. Born in Jammu in 1935, Pritam Singh adopted 'bridging nations'—India and Nepal—as his neeyat. Through transport, he would serve the people of these two nations. Pritam cites his inspiration as emanating from his father and his religion. He put into practice the tenets of Sikhism, but for the benefit of all of the society he served.

Gopal came upon another not-so-known but good example of sound neeyat from his many years of working in the Arabian Peninsula during the 1990s. Beit Binzagr was a business partner of Unilever. Naturally, Gopal developed quite a close working relationship with the Binzagr brothers. Even the nomenclature of their institution, 'Beit' (Arabic for house) rather than 'Group', suggested the existence and continuity of congruent values and ethics within the institution.

The Binzagr family originally hailed from the Hadramauth area of Yemen—the word literally means 'the plateau'. The Hadramauthis are a tribe well-known for their sound trading practices, a bit like the Tamil Chettiars or Kutchi Bhatias in India. The Binzagr trading business began with one of the ancestors settling in Jeddah around the mid-1800s. Beit Binzagr has now been active and flourishing for close to a century and a half.

Its longevity in itself suggests that the firm may have been founded in a broth of good principles. According to the research done by Family Business Centre, the average life of a family-owned business is estimated to be only twenty-four years, so 150 is indeed long.

It is pertinent to point out that during the 1800s, the Kingdom of Saudi Arabia had not been founded. Jeddah was an important part of the Ottoman empire. During the one and a half centuries of the life of Beit Binzagr, Saudi Arabia went from being one of the poorest regions of the world to among the richest. The nation also transformed into an independent kingdom from being part of the mighty Ottoman empire.

Beit Binzagr enjoyed long-standing relations with several international companies—for example, Unilever, Hershey's, Carlsberg and Heinz. Just as it happens within a society, nation or institution, if relationships among the members are managed effectively, then the institution prospers.

As a family-managed business, Beit Binzagr laid great store on managing differences and enhancing commonalities between all their partners. Gopal had for long reckoned that this internal glue of Beit Binzagr must have been a key element of the institution's neeyat. As modern management experts would say, no one is smarter than all of us put together. Beit Binzagr's stated values are (i) integrity (acting responsibly and transparently)), (ii) collaboration (partnerships of mutual respect), (iii) empowerment (consulting and taking ownership of decisions), (iv) agility (adapting to change) and (v) performance (continuous learning and development). No wonder they transformed from trading to manufacturing to serving 15,000 customers each day, month after month, currently achieving revenues of hundreds of millions of dollars.

This admirable trait that Gopal sensed in Beit Binzagr taught him many lessons on handling differences and achieving goal alignment.

Neeyat is not a piece of new management jargon to replace vision and mission. Commonplace, not-so-popular stories are evidence that neeyat is relevant for all enterprises, small and big, family-run, promoter-driven or multinational.

Indeed, the House of Tata was founded by Jamsetji in 1868, when India was a British colony, and has prospered through colonialism, Independence, Partition, socialism and liberalization to present times. Its neeyat, or purpose, has remained substantially unchanged, though the language and expression describing it have been modernized periodically. To remain constant to a single purpose and also be perceived as faithful to its original values for so long—save for the occasional frailties and controversies—is an achievement that is instructive and inspiring for all entrepreneurs.

The stories that follow adduce to the importance of the first of the several Ps that make Jamsetji still relevant—purpose.

Stories of Purpose

1. A Silk Farm for the Community

Jamsetji Tata travelled extensively across the world, primarily with the purpose of bringing back the best ideas and technologies to the country of his birth, India. During his visits to France and Italy, he noticed with interest that silk was highly valued in these European countries. A thought came to his mind—could the manufacture of silk benefit his own country and create employment for Indians? This was a cottage industry, and therefore appeared well suited to the India of that time. His countrymen were poor. They needed jobs and income. Here was an opportunity to build an industry that could provide some of these jobs.

In 1893, he visited Japan for discussions relating to a new shipping venture. Here he saw that the Japanese had developed the silk industry very well, based on scientific principles, and were even ahead of the Europeans. In particular, as he was shown the ways in which the Japanese had developed silk cultivation, he was deeply impressed.

It is likely that he stood in the Japanese silk farms and wondered at their mastery of this art, including the manner in which they had prepared the soil for sericulture.

During this visit, he became convinced that he could build a thriving silk industry in India. What he needed was a location with a temperate climate, which was suited to sericulture, and the help of Japanese experts. He identified a Japanese husband-and-wife couple, who had the required expertise, and invited them to come to India. In addition, he appointed a Japanese man called Odzu, who was then in the service of his cousin R.D. Tata and also knew English, as an interpreter. Throughout this time his mind was grappling with the question—Where in India should his new silk farm be located?

When Jamsetji returned to India, he decided to establish this farm in the state of Mysore, where a silk industry had flourished in the distant past, but unfortunately had declined over the centuries. In addition, he knew the dewan of Mysore, Sir Sheshadri Iyer, who was generally open to such progressive ventures. The city that was chosen for the silk farm was Bangalore. It was selected primarily for its temperate climate. Bangalore is better known today as the information technology and start-up capital of India, but in those days it was still a sleepy little town not far from the capital city of Mysore.

Jamsetji presented his proposal to the Mysore government, and he was granted the land required to commence this venture. This land was located in the far south of Bangalore city, near the area which is today called Basavanagudi. It was soon planted with many varieties of the mulberry bush. Jamsetji invested the required capital for all key aspects, such as cultivation of the mulberry bushes, rearing of the silkworm, treatment of any diseases that may impact its development, import of the reeling machinery from Japan and the eventual post-cultivation processing and packaging for European markets, where it would obtain a very good price.

The silk farm was established soon, and work began at a quick pace. The imported reeling equipment was installed under the instructions of the Japanese couple. At the centre of the farm's operations was the employment it generated for the local people. Apprentices were taken into the farm and provided training for at least three months, free of charge. This was at the heart of one of Jamsetji's dreams for his nation—creating experts in silk cultivation and processing. They were trained in every single area—cultivation of the bush, rearing and cross-breeding of silkworms, early detection of disease, preservation of cocoons, processing of silk and its packaging for exports.

The Indian trainees proved more than equal to the task. With the training they received from the Japanese couple, they were able to generate raw silk that was of such high quality that European experts said it was the best Indian silk they had ever seen. This was a vindication of Jamsetji's belief that Indians could deliver excellent products that would be appreciated across the world. The Tata Silk Farm soon became a big success, and this in turn encouraged the government of India to consider establishing similar farms at other locations in the country.

A letter that Jamsetji Tata wrote to the inspector general of agriculture on 16 April 1903 highlighted his key objective in establishing the silk farm. He wrote:

The principal keynote that has impressed me much in
your letter is that you have as your principal aim to
train picked natives of the country in all departments of
science and agriculture. Such should be the end-object
of all sympathetic persons who are at the head of all
Government Departments. I have always in my limited
sphere endeavoured to keep to this aim of training the
native talent, and am always prepared to offer all the
help and facility to those who so deserve it.

After Jamsetji Tata passed away in 1904, his son Dorabji
Tata, who succeeded him as chairman of the Tata Group,
got very busy implementing the large industrial dreams
of his father—the steel company and the hydroelectric
power company, as well as India's first university of
higher education and research in science, which Jamsetji
had envisioned. In the midst of these gigantic ventures,
Dorabji could not devote adequate time to the silk farm. In
1910, he wrote to the Salvation Army, requesting them to
take over the project, with the due consent of the Mysore
government. The Salvation Army agreed to do so.

A booklet published by the Salvation Army
headquarters in 1912, authored by F. Booth Tucker,
talks about the significant impetus that the Tata Silk
Farm had provided to the Indian silk industry:

Villagers are students [who] have been trained in
the Japanese system of reeling and re-reeling silk.
A cheap and convenient reeling machine has been
manufactured for cottage use. The acreage of mulberry
has been considerably increased, several new buildings

have been erected and a number of basins doubled in the filature. Visitors from different parts of India have called, and advice has been sought by numerous correspondents.

Already the Tata Silk Farm has given birth to three other Institutions of a similar character under our auspices in Ceylon, the United Provinces and the Punjab.

Thus the aim and object of its founder, that the Tata Silk Farm should be a Pan-Indian character, is already being realised.

During the past few months, this Institution has been awarded a Gold Medal in Bangalore and a silver medal in Madras for its exhibit of the entire process from the silkworm egg to the woven article.

A small weaving school under a trained weaving master now forms a part of this interesting Institution which is at present still in its infancy, but which possesses in it the nucleus of great future possibilities.

In fact, some of the giants of Indian sericulture, such as Appadorai Mudaliar and Laxman Rao, were amongst the Tata Silk Farm's first trainees.

The Salvation Army successfully enlarged the Tata Silk Farm, and it soon became a model for the entire country. Highlighting this positive impact, F. Booth Tucker wrote in 1912 to Burjorji Padshah, a close associate of Jamsetji Tata and later a Tata director:

The impetus thus given to the silk industry in India can hardly be over-estimated. The Government, which

before had given up the effort in despair, have now
recommenced operations. Orders have been issued for
the general planting of mulberry trees and bushes . . . In
the not distant days when silk will have become to India
what it already is in such countries as Japan, China,
France and Italy, the name of the man who launched
the enterprise will be held in grateful remembrance by
those who will have been benefited by his forethought
and labours.

Many years later, the original silk farm was converted into
a vegetable farm to feed an orphanage. Today it no longer
exists, but the locals still fondly refer to the entire area as
the 'Tata Silk Farm'.

Today, Mysore silk is very well known and enjoys an
excellent reputation. The Central Silk Board, established
in Bangalore in 1949, has taken on the role of evangelizing
the development and growth of the silk industry in India.

But as we look back on the Tata Silk Farm, an
experiment launched by Jamsetji Tata, we see in it the clear
imprint of the purpose that he wished to achieve—creation
of an industry that India could be proud of, skilling Indians
and generating sustained employment for them.

2. Cancer Care for the Country

On 29 April 2022, the prime minister of India, Narendra
Modi, inaugurated seven cancer-care facilities in Assam, in
the north-east of India. These seven hospitals were located
in the far-flung towns of Dibrugarh, Barpeta, Kokrajhar,
Lakhimpur, Darrang, Jorhat and Tezpur. For the people of

these towns, this was a godsend. Cancer patients and their families would no longer have to worry about travelling to far-off locations for treatment, and the often unbearable expenses that this would entail.

The facilities were a joint initiative of the Tata Trusts and the Government of Assam, an integral part of a network of world-class hospitals being set up across the state to address the scourge of cancer, which is very prevalent in this region. In fact, in addition to these seven hospitals, Prime Minister Modi also laid the foundation stones for the next set of seven hospitals too. Ratan Tata, chairman of the Tata Trusts, and N. Chandrasekaran, chairman of Tata Sons, were present at this event.

Here is what Ratan Tata said on this occasion:

I am happy that the Tata Trusts, along with the state Government's support, has been able to implement the multi-level cancer care network in Assam. Cancer care in India is challenged by lack of facilities, late diagnosis and high cost of treatment. The Tata Trusts have resolved to combat this by supporting the creation of capabilities across the country for high quality affordable care, nation-wide screening and early detection programmes. The fruition of this project in Assam will be a guiding light to the entire country.

Indeed, for the Tata Trusts, the fight against cancer is not just a major initiative but an abiding mission, an undertaking that has evolved over more than eighty years. To know the origins of this story, we must go back in time to an ocean liner that was sailing the mighty Pacific, way back in the

year 1933. Sir Nowroji Saklatvala, who had succeeded Sir
Dorabji Tata as chairman of the Tata Group, was travelling
on this ship. Also on the ship was Dr John Spies, a cancer
expert who had worked at the Sloan Kettering Memorial in
the USA, one of the best-known cancer-care institutes in the
world. He was now heading a cancer facility in China.

This was a long sea voyage. Sir Nowroji and Dr Spies
got talking on board the ship. Sir Nowroji mentioned to Dr
Spies how his predecessor, Sir Dorabji Tata, had considered
the establishment of a radium institute in Mumbai, to help
treat cancer. Dorabji's beloved wife, Lady Meherbai Tata,
had died of leukaemia in 1931, and this had spurred him to
consider such a facility. However, Dorabji had passed away
soon thereafter, before he could take forward this proposal.

At that time, India had no cancer hospital of its
own, and Sir Nowroji was keen to bring to fruition his
predecessor's dream, which would greatly benefit the
nation. He requested Dr Spies to provide his observations
on how best such a facility should be created. Dr Spies
agreed, and he soon provided a comprehensive report,
which recommended that, for best results, all methods of
treatment should be available in a single hospital. This
would mean a comprehensive hospital, and not just a
radium facility.

Such a comprehensive hospital would entail significant
expenditure for its establishment, and also long-term
financial commitment for its operation. The Dorabji
Tata Trust was faced with a huge hospital project that
was much larger than any such venture ever undertaken
by a private organization in India. In 1937, Sir Nowroji
reported to the Trust, 'Our hospital budget has gone up

out of all proportions. Naturally, Dr Spies wants to put up the hospital on a very modern scale which requires serious thought.' In the meanwhile, the Second World War broke out, placing further constraints on the project. There was great doubt as to whether the project would move forward.

Notwithstanding these issues, the Dorabji Tata Trust took a bold call to commit to this ambitious cancer hospital project. In coming to this decision, it is very likely that the trustees, who included Sir Nowroji and J.R.D. Tata, and the managing trustee J.D. Ghandhy, bore in mind the purpose for which the Tata Group had been established—to be of service to the community. What better area of service than provision of critical medical facilities that could help save and extend human lives?

Dr Clifford Manshardt, who served as director of the Dorabji Tata Trust between 1936 and 1941, has recorded one of the intense conversations on this subject, which illustrates the determination with which the project was approved and pursued.

The Managing Trustee of the Trust at that time was Mr J.D. Ghandhy—a man over eighty years of age, but mentally alert as a man of forty. I remember one day in his office when a committee of Bombay doctors advised us against undertaking the radium project on the ground that it was too difficult. Mr Ghandhy turned to me and exploded—'Difficult? Did Jamsetji Tata ever quit because of difficulties? We will go ahead!'

And so, the cancer hospital project went ahead. The Tata Trusts made a capital grant of Rs 30 lakh, a huge sum in those days, to fund the hospital. Even with these funds in place, it was an incredibly difficult project to execute. Dr Manshardt writes:

> Only those who were associated with the hospital project during the years of its planning will know the amount of hard work which went into the making of the Tata Memorial Hospital. Only those who shared in the ups-and-downs, the disappointments and the successes, can realise the human anguish that went into the Institution . . . An undertaking of the magnitude of the Tata Memorial Hospital would have been difficult in any country, but to rear an institution of this kind, in the face of limitations under which we were working in Bombay, required imagination, energy, patience, pertinacity and obstinacy.

Eventually, in 1941, the hospital was completed and was inaugurated by the governor of Bombay, Sir Roger Lumley. The facility included operating theatres, research laboratories and lecture rooms. The departments of surgery, pathology, radiology, radiophysics and anaesthesia were all in place. Except for two American surgeons, all the staff were proudly and entirely Indian. Asia's and India's first comprehensive cancer-care hospital was now open to the public.

Today this hospital is supported and managed by the Department of Atomic Energy of the Government of India. Over 64,000 patients visit it every year. Around 70 per cent of these patients receive treatment free of charge. The doctors in this hospital are revered by patients and their families, because they do the work of God.

In recent years, the Tata Trusts have continued the fight against cancer with admirable energy, under the leadership of Ratan Tata. In 2011, the Tata Medical Centre was established at Kolkata to address the lack of suitable facilities in eastern India. This is an integrated oncology facility with over 400 beds, and 75 per cent of its infrastructure is earmarked for subsidized treatment for underprivileged sections of society. It provides a wide spectrum of services, ranging from complete diagnosis to multimodality therapy, prehabilitation to rehabilitation, psycho-oncological support to palliative care. The objective is very clear—to excel in cancer care, patient service, education and research. The hospital has already made a deep impact, with the help of cutting-edge technology and world-renowned healthcare professionals.

The seven cancer-care hospitals inaugurated in Assam, which have been referred to at the start of this story, are only the latest outposts on this mission. The future roadmap of the Tata Trusts is equally ambitious. It includes the setting up of cancer care and treatment centres at many other locations in the country, including Varanasi, Tirupati, Bhubaneshwar, Ranchi, Allahabad and Mangaluru. The trusts are also partnering with the state governments of Odisha, Jharkhand, Telangana and Nagaland for cancer-care facilities in these states.

The continuing establishment of these facilities re-emphasize the words of Sir Sorab Saklatvala, who served as chairman of the Dorabji Tata Trust between 1938 and 1948, as he reflected on the Tata Memorial Hospital in Mumbai. He mentioned that the hospital was a temple of learning, where doctors would work hard to 'wrest from this dreaded scourge some of its terrible secrets'. And then he went on to say: 'It is a task in which many men have faithfully laboured, inspired with the hope that in doing so they set their hands on a project which may well spell happiness and good health to many millions of their fellowmen.'

3. Lakes, Trees and Trucks

The huge manufacturing plant of Tata Motors located in the Pimpri-Chinchwad area of Pune is a landmark in the city. If you visit this plant, you will find a modern manufacturing facility that makes vehicles ranging from trucks to SUVs to cars. There are halls full of robots, and assembly lines through which gleaming new vehicles pass. The plant has been, and continues to be, a showcase of India's manufacturing prowess.

But you will also be delighted to discover that just opposite this plant there is a big lake. The lake is surrounded by thick clumps of lush green trees. Should you pause here for a moment, you will also see a number of beautiful migratory birds, which have come all the way from places such as Siberia. And you will perhaps be surprised to hear that this is not a natural water body. It is an artificial lake, created simultaneously with the Tata Motors manufacturing plant.

Here is the fascinating story of this lake, and why it was created.

In the 1960s, Tata Motors (or TELCO, as it was then called) decided to create a second manufacturing plant to add to its original plant located in Jamshedpur. The company foresaw a boom in the automobile industry and wanted to add significant capacity to be able to cater to this demand. Pune was chosen as the location of this new plant. Over 800 acres of barren and rocky land were acquired for this project.

Sumant Moolgaokar, the then managing director of the company, led this venture, and his objective was to create a world-class facility that the country could be proud of. He was of the view that the company should not merely assemble or make vehicles, it should also have the capability to design its own machinery, dyes and press-tools so that it has intrinsic manufacturing strength.

In addition, he did something remarkable. He felt that the unit should give back to nature and not merely take from it. Looking at the barren land in front of him, he had the factory designed in such a way that there were large open spaces left all along the roads and the production units. Then he decided to plant over 2.5 lakh trees within the factory campus, to ensure adequate greenery alongside the manufacturing halls. He wanted to create a complex that 'looks more like a tree park than a factory site', and which provided a harmonious, clean work environment to the factory community.

To ensure that this is done in the best possible manner, he uniquely went ahead and appointed a chief horticulturist for the plant, alongside automobile and design engineers. M.D. Sharma, the man who was appointed to this role, recalls that Moolgaokar discussed the horticultural programme of the Pune factory in as much detail as he discussed the manufacturing blueprints: 'He liked specific trees like the pipal, banyan, kadamba, jambool and other traditional native trees on account of their big size and therefore their capacity for purifying the air and also for their bird attracting qualities.'

Moolgaokar was criticized by some for spending significant additional money on this large-scale planting of trees and associated works, but he was unfazed. In fact, he was adamant that the factory should give back as much as it could to the community. Therefore, he went a step ahead. All these trees would require water, so he decided to create an artificial lake that could store and provide water throughout the year. And then he also envisioned the creation of a water-bird sanctuary for migratory birds at this lake, by planting a forest all around.

Here is a beautiful description of how the lake and the bird sanctuary were created, in the words of the chief horticulturist M.D. Sharma himself:

Telco's famous water bird sanctuary was created on about 100 acres of a part of the residential land adjacent to the factory site. This was his (Moolgaokar's) brainchild. As necessary infrastructure, he had a stone masonry dam built in 1967 across a nullah to trap rain water, which ultimately resulted in the creation of a large lake capable of holding 60 million gallons of water, and which also supplies over one lakh gallons of water daily to the tree plantations. In the following years, several ponds and a second lake were added to this complex by nullah bunding. This also enabled us to grow a dense forest around these water bodies through a massive afforestation program.

This is today regarded as the best bird sanctuary in the Pune region for thousands of migratory water birds it attracts during winter, besides serving as a permanent habitat for hundreds of resident birds and other common wildlife such as partridges, quails, rabbits, etc.

In one fell stroke, Sumant Moolgaokar had created not merely a world-class manufacturing plant but also an equally admirable plantation and lake that would add back to the community for decades afterwards.

Moolgaokar was criticized for spending Rs 15 lakh to create this lake. Today this man-made wetland has over 1.5 lakh trees and has also supplied thousands of fruit trees to surrounding villages through a nursery that has been established. It is a beautiful haven for over 150 species of migratory birds and sixty types of butterflies. It is celebrated as a green oasis within the city.

In the meanwhile, the new Tata Motors plant at Pune has manufactured many modern vehicles which have contributed meaningfully to transport, mobility and logistics in our country. The lake, the trees and the trucks all belong together.

As J.R.D Tata once said about this fascinating initiative, 'We did not have to create a lake and plant trees to produce a truck. But we did. What I am most proud about is not the making of steel or trucks, but our social concern.'

3

Pioneering

'When you have to give the lead in action, in ideas—a lead which does not fit in with the very climate of opinion, that is true courage, physical or mental or spiritual, call it what you like, and it is this kind of courage and vision that Jamsetji Tata showed, and that it is right that we should honour his memory and remember him as one of the big founders of modern India'—Jawaharlal Nehru at the inauguration of Jubilee Park, Jamshedpur, 1 March 1958.

Jamsetji Tata had many illustrious contemporaries. Abroad there were pioneers like Thomas Edison, Andrew Carnegie, William Hesketh Lever and John Cadbury, to name a few. Within colonial India, his contemporaries were names like Dadabhai Naoroji, Pherozeshah Mehta, Rabindranath Tagore and Swami Vivekananda.

In his chosen field of pioneering entrepreneurship, Jamsetji was a leader par excellence. It is appropriate to view him as a giant who played a unique role in the development and birth of free India. He did not live to see a free India, but he contributed greatly to laying the foundations for it in his own sphere of influence. As referred to in the prologue of this book, these considerations must have prompted historian Ramachandra Guha to suggest that Jamsetji must count as among the greatest Indians of the nineteenth century.

There are three stories in this chapter about the sustained and pioneering entrepreneurship of the Tata leaders over the period of a century and more.

The first is from the early years. Jamsetji had the vision of setting up India's pioneering hydroelectric power generation stations in the Western Ghats. As Jamsetji's son Dorabji said at the inauguration of the Tata Hydroelectric Works on 11 February 1915:

To my father, the hydro-electric project was not merely
a dividend-earning scheme; it was a means to an
end . . . the development of the manufacturing power
of Bombay . . . The great sums of money needed were
forthcoming mainly because those who commanded
them believed the scheme would assuredly play an
important part in the industrial renaissance of India.

The second story concerns the creation of Tata Airlines. In
the environment prevalent in colonial India in 1920–1930,
starting an airline must have been considered a preposterous
idea. After all, the Wright brothers had proven the idea
of a flying machine at Kitty Hawk just twenty-five years
earlier. During his stint as a director at the Tata Group,
Gopal learnt that an initial proposal in 1929 to start an
airline had been rejected by the Tata Sons board. The
story describes how young JRD approached the problem
through his mentor, John Peterson, who was influential
with Dorabji Tata. 'Let the young man fly,' Peterson had
said to Dorabji. And JRD did! Later, the board gave its
approval for the airline.

History rhymes, and then repeats itself. It may be
appropriate to mention a subsequent incident. In 1968,
when J.R.D Tata was the chairman of the Tata Group,
Massachusetts Institute of Technology (MIT)-returned
engineer Faqir Chand Kohli approached the board to
support the group's entry into computers and software
(the future Tata Consultancy Services). It had been only
a decade before, in 1956, that William Shockley, John
Bardeen and Walter Brittain had won the Nobel Prize for
the invention of transistors, the key component that made

computers possible. The Tatas approved Kohli's proposal and went ahead.

Another thirty years after the pioneering decision on computers, Ratan Tata pioneered the idea of a totally indigenous passenger car, designed, developed and built, ground up, by the group. It would appear that till then, no Indian industrialist had thought of it, or, to be more accurate, nobody actually had done it, even if the idea did exist in somebody's mind. Gopal was privileged to attend, as a guest, the launch of the Tata Indica on 30 December 1998. It was a momentous day and an authentic continuation of the philosophy of pioneering. This is the third story that follows this chapter.

In this essay, pioneering is a word that connotes risk-taking and advocacy among those whose support was necessary for the venture in question. Human progress must be viewed in the context in which the act of pioneering is undertaken. The world in which Jamsetji pioneered hydroelectric power was different from today's. And so too when JRD pioneered an airline. Both these ventures were undertaken when India was a poor country under colonial domination. Indica was pioneered in the early days of liberalization, which itself happened after several decades of inward-looking socialistic industrial policies. It is pertinent to recall that in the 1980s, a Tata proposal to set up a joint venture with Honda to make passenger cars did not find favour with the government of the day!

Nowadays India celebrates itself as a start-up nation. In earlier times, everything was deficient for the entrepreneur—policy support, capital, skilled manpower, foreign exchange, access to modern machinery . . . you name it.

A brief comment on the policy and capital environment during the time of the Tatas venturing into mega capital-intensive projects in steel, hydro-power may be of interest. To ignore the difficulties of the initial stages would be to do Jamsetji a grave injustice. In February 1899, in an interview with the *Ceylon Independent*, Jamsetji reflected on the obstacles posed by colonial rule: 'If some Englishmen treated us more considerately, there would be more harmony than there is . . . It is in the clubs and institutions that a certain amount of antipathy is stirred up.' Indeed, the then chief commissioner of Indian Railways, Sir Frederick Upcott, famously said, 'Do you say that Tatas propose to make steel rails to British specifications? Why, I will undertake to eat every pound of steel rail they succeed in making.'

Jamsetji must have discussed with fellow industrialists, lawyers and friends in his own Ripon Club about the obstreperous attitude of the British officers. The Ripon Club still stands on the third and fourth floors of N.M. Wadia building on Mahatma Gandhi Road in Mumbai. The furniture there makes one wonder whether time has stood still at the club. One of the authors, Gopal, had visited this club to absorb the sights and smells that Jamsetji must have experienced, though being a vegetarian, he did not savour its famous mutton dhansak buffet. Even today, on Wednesday afternoons, one can see at the Ripon Club its Parsi members, young and old, resting on easy chairs after a sumptuous dhansak lunch!

The club was founded by the likes of Sir Pherozeshah Mehta, Sir Dinshaw Petit and, of course, Jamsetji Tata. Jamsetji had constructed his own private residence opposite what is now the Bombay Gymkhana, and it was under a mile of a ride to the Ripon Club in his horse-drawn carriage. Jamsetji named his elegant house Esplanade House, perhaps since that area was called the Esplanade in those times.

And, of course, bang opposite the Ripon Club stood the luxurious Watson's Esplanade Hotel. This elegant building was the first cast-iron structure in India. It was prefabricated in England and shipped to Bombay. In 1896, Lumiere Brothers screened short films for the first time in India at the Esplanade Hotel.

According to the unverifiable folklore of the city, the hotel denied Jamsetji entry with his European guest because he was an Indian! Whether that incident is true or not, it is a fact that the elegant Taj Mahal hotel was inaugurated within a few years to cater to people of all faiths and nationalities. Alas, the long-unoccupied Watson Hotel building is now in a shambles, and is currently being reconditioned by the municipality.

The colonial government was incredulous, if not suspicious, of the aspirations of Jamsetji to set up a steel plant, generate hydro-electricity and provide an institution of higher learning and science. Jamsetji was born in 1839 and was a teenager during the throes of India's first war of independence, as Veer Savarkar would call it, or the Indian Mutiny, as the British would call it. The Bessemer process was the first inexpensive steel process that allowed mass production of steel, and a patent was awarded for the process in 1856. The first electric lighting demonstration in India was in 1882, at Crawford Market in Bombay. The first automobile was brought to Bombay in 1897, followed by four more cars in 1898. One of those four cars belonged to Jamsetji. It was a different world, in which for sure Jamsetji must have been viewed as foolishly ambitious.

Raising funds was ridiculously tough. Dadabhai Naoroji had advised Jamsetji to talk to Indian business leaders. The National Archives contains a letter written by Jamsetji to Dadabhai Naoroji dated 22 April 1885 in which he states: 'I have got Nathooram Poddar on my list for Rs 200, but unfortunately, he is one of only two I have been able to secure.' Their correspondence continued, and on 16 September 1902, Dadabhai replied: 'Is it not possible to raise the million you want from the Indian Princes?' Just five days later, Dadabhai Naoroji seemed to despair, 'It is quite futile for me to say anything more. Poor India is still pursued by the same misfortune by which her own children with their own blood and money handed her over to the heaviest of all yokes—the yoke of the stranger.' ('Yoke of the Stranger' was an earlier remark by Macaulay about the 'natives'!)

Other Pioneers

It is instructive to briefly consider the experiences of Jamsetji's steel contemporary, Andrew Carnegie, in pioneering the industry in his country. Carnegie's life was a history of pursuit of cutting-edge technology in the nineteenth century. He saw his father's business in handmade textiles rendered irrelevant by the entry of steam-powered looms. When the telegraph arrived, Carnegie mastered its craft. When the railroad revolution took place, he turned out to be in the right place at the right time. When the Bessemer steel process arrived,

Carnegie was there to adopt it. As an enterprise builder, Carnegie's defining characteristic seems to have been a combination of foresight and a welcoming of change. After all, it is hard to know the future and the ways of the market, as much as it is humanly comforting to avoid jettisoning the past.

Was Carnegie simply lucky? Or did fortune favour the brave? Or was he fond of embracing the future rather than the past, when most people are prone to doing the opposite? Perhaps it was a bit of all three.

Jamsetji also demonstrated these characteristics. Jamsetji began his career with trading. The faraway American Civil War opened up a huge opportunity for the export of cotton from colonial India. The colonial government discouraged the Indian manufacture of fabric to protect Britain's own Lancashire economy. Jamsetji went into textile manufacture, with the latest ring spindle technology to boot. Then in London, he heard a speech by Thomas Carlyle prophesying that the country which would have steel would have gold. Jamsetji displayed a single-minded focus to prospect for iron ore, find the world's best technologists and raise funds, surmounting the obstacles all along on his way to putting up a steel plant in India.

Just as Arjuna in the Mahabharata was considered 'savya sachi'—multi-dexterous—Jamsetji displayed 'savya sachi' skills by simultaneously dreaming about hydro-electric power and a higher institute of science. It must be a characteristic of pioneers to do diametrically opposite things simultaneously—focus on tasks as well as scan for opportunity, imagine as well as execute, and embrace the future without sacrificing the past.

Through the three stories that follow, it is interesting to observe how the pioneering 'BHAG' approach—big, hairy, audacious goals—has characterized the Tata approach to entrepreneurship over the decades. The first story concerns the hydroelectric project of the early 1900s, the second is about Tata Airlines in the 1930s and the third is about Tata Indica in the 1990s. It is worthwhile to note how the pioneering spirit was preserved in successive leaders of the Tata Group.

Stories of Pioneering

1. Lighting Up Lives

As early as 1875, Jamsetji Tata had considered exploring the use of hydraulic energy for his first greenfield industrial venture, Empress Mills. While this particular idea did not eventually fructify, he retained his keen interest in the use of clean energy for commercial purposes. Around twenty years later, in 1897, his latent interest in the subject blossomed when an engineer, David Gostling, put forward to Jamsetji a proposal for the development of hydroelectric energy in the Western Ghats. These ghats receive heavy monsoon rainfall, and their hills with their sharp gradients make them ideal for hydroelectric projects.

Jamsetji grasped the immense possibilities of such a project immediately. He had experienced the benefit of using electric drives in his textile mills, and two strategic advantages stood out for him. First, hydroelectric power would reduce the industry's dependence on expensive coal. Second, it would also purify the environment, because the use of coal led to soot and pollution within the mills, whereas electricity generated from water was clean. He appears to have concluded that this was a valuable business opportunity that would also contribute positively to the community.

Having reached this conclusion, he moved forward with determination and thoughtfulness. Never before had such an ambitious hydroelectric project been undertaken in the country. He first applied himself to the detailing of the scheme. After this, he approached the British government of India to secure the required land and licence. He also travelled to London in 1902 and spoke directly to the Secretary of State for India, Lord George Hamilton, putting forward his scheme lucidly and passionately. Lord George was impressed with the possibilities of the project, and provided his support to it.

Unfortunately, Jamsetji Tata fell ill within a year of this meeting and passed away in 1904. His son, Dorabji Tata, inherited his mantle as Chairman of the Tata Group. Dorabji was determined to bring to a successful conclusion his father's big dreams for India, including the hydro-electric project. Much like his father, he was also a man of determination and persistence. He enlisted the help of experts, including David Gostling, who surveyed the area accurately, and R.B. Joyner, who focused on the design of dams. With their help, technical work progressed well, despite there being no precedent in the country for a hydro-electric project of the magnitude they were attempting.

Dorabji was also able to obtain big and reliable customers for the project well in advance. Two of Mumbai's largest mill owners—Sir David Sassoon and Sir Shapurji Broacha—guaranteed the purchase of significant amounts of electric power from this project.

There was a problem, though. Dorabji had to raise a significant quantum of funds for the project. Unfortunately, at that time (around 1905 to 1910) a financial crisis in America had depressed markets, and liquidity was tight. Initial attempts to raise money from the foreign market were futile. The project went through a very difficult phase, barely staying alive.

However, at this juncture, unexpected support came from an unlikely source. Lord Sydenham, the Governor of Bombay, was also an engineer by training and he had developed a keen enthusiasm for the project. Speaking at the opening of a cotton mill in Sholapur in 1910, he told his audience,

> There is an excellent hydro electric project for Bombay, which awaits initiation. Experience has shown the great value of cheap electricity in connection with a growing city . . . and it was my great hope that the scheme could be launched entirely upon Indian capital. There are obvious advantages in carrying out such a scheme as a purely Indian undertaking, and I regret that I see no hopes that this can be arranged.

These words had an immediate impact on the audience. There was an upswell of support in India for funding the project. Dorabji Tata visited various states in the country and obtained promises of financing support. As he said a year later, 'From that point we never looked back. We were filled with hope and our optimism was justified by the launching of the company in November 1910.'

Indeed, on 7 November 1910, the Tata Hydro Electric Supply Company was registered as a public concern. On

8 February 1911, the foundation stone of the first dam, at Walwhan, was laid. This was a momentous occasion. At this event, highlighting the purpose behind this venture, Dorabji Tata said: 'To my father the acquisition of wealth was only a secondary object in his life. It was always subordinate to the constant desire in his heart to improve the industrial and intellectual condition of the people of this country.'

Lord Sydenham was also present, and he said of the project, 'It symbolizes the confidence of Indians in themselves, their willingness to be associated with a project somewhat unfamiliar in this country and their assurance of the political stability, which alone can guarantee the continual advancement of India.'

Work began immediately on the construction of the Walwhan dam, which was a commendable engineering feat. This marvellous dam, when completed, stood at a height of 86.5 feet, with a length of 4449 feet and a dam volume of 64,00,000 cubic feet. It was only a little smaller than the original legendary dam on the Nile at Aswan constructed by Sir William Wilcocks. Many people had thought that such a massive scheme was inconceivable in India, but the Tatas were determined to make it happen.

Around the same time, two more adjacent dams were built by the company—at Lonavala and Shirawta. Giant pipes were laid, around 7 feet in diameter, to carry water from all these dams to the foot of the Western Ghats. Water rushed through these pipes, along a steep fall of 1,734 feet, to the power station at Khopoli. Here, hydraulic energy was converted into electric energy using massive generators. The electricity thus generated was initially transmitted to a receiving station in Mumbai, and thereon through transmission lines to the mills of Mumbai.

This was a complicated project involving many engineering challenges, including the construction of an artificial river, the laying of pipes that were hewn into the solid rocks of the hills, and the anchoring of these pipes to deal with issues arising from the tropical heat. Nothing of this magnitude had ever been attempted in the past in India. By any standards this was pioneering work.

Eventually, the engineering and construction work was completed in four years. On 11 February 1915, Lord Willingdon, who had now assumed charge as Governor of Bombay, switched on the power at the receiving station in Parel, a locality in Mumbai. Addressing Dorabji Tata, he said, 'It must be a source of pride and satisfaction to you, Mr Chairman, and to your brother, to find that you have established in India another magnificent and permanent memorial to your father's great services to his country.'

In one stroke these dams and hydroelectric projects provided clean power to drive more than one-third of all the mills in Mumbai. It was hoped that with this supply of hydroelectric power, Mumbai would soon become a 'smokeless city', free of the grimy coal that textile mills were burning at that time for their energy requirements. These mills also gained significantly from inexpensive electricity, thus bringing to life the exact goals for which Jamsetji Tata had visualized this project.

Today Tata Power, the company born at Walwhan over a century ago, continues to proudly supply uninterrupted power to the city of Mumbai. Here was a venture that was born in the mind of a great pioneer, Jamsetji Tata, and

executed to perfection by another pioneer, his son Dorabji
Tata. They went where no one had gone before, to construct
a magnificent project surpassing anything that had been
done in India until then. Multiple obstacles, including
engineering and financial challenges, were overcome with
sheer determination. It was a tribute to the ambition that
these great men had for the prosperity of India.

We can, to this day, take inspiration from Lord
Willingdon's words at the opening ceremony of the project.
He said:

> I cannot do better today than ask one and all to take as
> an example and inspiration for their future lives the life-
> work of Mr. Jamsetji Tata. If they strenuously endeavour
> to emulate his example, I am full of hope that in the
> future we may produce many men in this country with
> brains, character and courage, whose work will stand
> high in their various professions in all parts of the world.

2. A Pilot Turns Pioneer—the Making of an Airline

J.R.D. Tata was fascinated by aeroplanes since his
childhood. As a young boy he had lived for some time in the
small town of Hardelot in the north of France, which was
also home to the famous aviator Louis Bleriot. JRD was
fascinated by Bleriot and his aircraft. In his own words,
'From then on, I was hooked on aeroplanes and made up
my mind that come what may, one day I would be a pilot.
I had to wait for many years for that dream to come true.'

That dream eventually came true in 1929, when a
flying club opened in Bombay. JRD seized the opportunity,

and within the next three weeks had collected the required flying experience to obtain his pilot's licence. On 10 February 1929, he was issued his license; as he was the first individual to have qualified in India, his license bore the number 1. 'No document has ever given me a greater thrill,' J.R.D. Tata told his biographer R.M. Lala. Flying was indeed one of the great loves of his life.

Passion is a great thing to have, but pioneering is a completely different flight, as JRD would soon realize. Within a month of getting his flying license, JRD met with a remarkable aviator, a man named Neville Vintcent. He had served in the Royal Air Force for many years, and, apart from being a pilot, was also a heavyweight boxing champion. Now he was keen to start an airline that would service peninsular India. He put forward this proposal to JRD.

Young JRD (he was twenty-five years of age at that time) was excited, because he saw a real opportunity for civil aviation in India. It is likely that he saw this as a coming together of his passion, a business opportunity and a national need. However, in taking the idea forward, he faced his first challenge within the Tata Group itself. The Group was just recovering from some setbacks following the First World War, including withdrawals from some businesses after a string of expansions. This was not a conducive environment for broaching the topic of entry into a relatively new and risky area such as airlines. In addition, the Chairman of the Group, Sir Dorabji Tata, was known to be a tough nut to crack, and JRD did not have the best of relationships with him.

This was JRD's first test. He did something interesting. Rather than speaking to Sir Dorabji, he reached out to John

Peterson, the director in charge of Tata Steel, who was also his mentor and guide in the Group. He requested John for his help in convincing Sir Dorabji about the proposal. And then he held his breath while John Peterson entered the chairman's office in Bombay House to discuss the matter.

Peterson requested Sir Dorabji to permit the young JRD to take forward the airline project. Perhaps because Peterson enjoyed the chairman's confidence, and also because he was a persuasive man, Sir Dorabji finally agreed, on the specific understanding that the initial foray would cost a relatively small sum of Rs 2 lakh. JRD had crossed the first milestone.

Now began the long and arduous process of obtaining approvals from the British government of India. The Tata Group also requested the Government for a subsidy of Rs 1.25 lakh, but this was summarily refused it. For the next two years, the British government kept this proposal in abeyance, despite a lot of repeated correspondence and contact. JRD was on tenterhooks as he waited to hear whether the government would permit an Indian company to enter the field of civil aviation in the country. He also feared that the board of Tata Sons would run out of patience. In the meanwhile, Neville Vintcent, running out of hope, accepted another job offer, though he agreed to return to lead the Tata aviation project as and when it was approved.

Eventually, in 1932, after having dragged their feet for a long time, the government approved the Tata proposal for an airline, and a ten-year contract was signed subject to some conditions, which included the proviso that the airline should only use British-made aircraft unless otherwise specifically permitted. JRD was relieved. He went across to England to purchase the two Puss Moth aircraft with which the enterprise would begin its operations. Interestingly, he was scheduled to fly back on one of these planes to India, but he could not do so because he fell ill. So he brought the aeroplane back to India by ship, as part of his personal baggage. That is how Air India's first aircraft reached the shores of our country!

The airline was not called Air India though, in those early days. It began its life as Tata Aviation Service. As with any pioneering venture, it had to contend with many unique challenges. For instance, Bombay did not have an airport in those days, so the first flight of this airline had to take off from the mud flats of Juhu, one of the city's fishing villages. There were no navigational or landing aids, either on the ground or in the air. There was no radio messaging. Notwithstanding these circumstances, the first Tata flight took off confidently from Karachi on 15 October 1932, soaring into the skies and heading towards Mumbai via Ahmedabad.

JRD piloted this flight himself. The great joy of being a pioneer emerges so beautifully in his reflections which he shared many years later:

> On an exciting October dawn in 1932, a Puss Moth and I soared joyfully from Karachi with our first precious load of air mail, on an inaugural flight to Bombay. As we hummed towards our destination at a 'dazzling' hundred miles an hour, I breathed a silent prayer for the success of our venture and for the safety of those who would work for it. We were a small team in those days. We

shared successes and failures, the joys and heartaches,
as together we built up the enterprise which was later to
blossom into Air India and Air India International.

And indeed it did blossom beautifully into a world-class
airline, under JRD's constant watch. In its very first year
of operations, it achieved 100 per cent punctuality, leading
the Directorate of Civil Aviation to hold it up as an example
of how an airmail service should be run. By 1934 it was
making profits without any subsidy from the government.
It expanded its routes and also quickly transformed from
an air mail service into carrying passengers too. In 1938,
J.R.D. Tata became the chairman of the Tata Group.
Notwithstanding all the wide-ranging commitments that
were part of his new leadership role, he kept alive his active
interest in the airline venture.

In 1946, Tata Air Lines was renamed Air India—a proud
symbol of an India that was on the verge of independence.
Immediately after Independence, JRD's restless pioneering
spirit urged him once again to do something no other
Indian airline had done before—to fly international. In
1948, Air India International was incorporated, and its first
international flight, from Bombay to London, took off on 8
June that year. For JRD this was a 'great and stirring event'.
He says, 'Seeing the Indian flag displayed on both sides of
the *Malabar Princess* (the name of the Air India constellation
aircraft which undertook the first international flight) as she
stood proudly on the apron at the airports of Cairo, Geneva
and London, filled me with joy and emotion.'

In the fiercely competitive world of international
airlines, Air India soon made its mark, providing customers

with impeccable service. It is said that in those days residents of Geneva could set their watches as they saw the Air India flight land in their city—such was its punctuality. J.R.D. Tata relentlessly pushed for excellence in all aspects of the airline, telling his employees, 'I want to establish that there is no airline which is better liked by passengers, that is safer and more punctual, where the food and service in better and which sets a better image than Air India.' In 1968, when the *Daily Mail* of London published a survey of international airlines, Air India topped the list.

In 1953, Air India was nationalized by the Government of India, though J.R.D. Tata was invited to remain the chairman of the airline, a role he essayed to perfection for many years thereafter. If JRD had been alive today, he would surely have been overjoyed to see that Air India has now come back home to the Tata Group, which it did in 2022. Because, as Ratan Tata has written, 'Many of us who knew Jeh (JRD) intimately knew that Air India was as important to him as the industrial empire he headed. While he led the Tata empire with distinction, Air India was his personal creation and his personal passion.' Such is the story of true pioneers—they love and nurture the enterprises they create with all their heart.

3. Indica for India: The Nation's First Indigenous Car

Cars are products of intense desire. Cars are also symbols of patriotism and pride because they are an important marker of the advancement of a nation's engineering capabilities and manufacturing ecosystem. Brands like Toyota, Mercedes-

Benz, Ford, Hyundai, Fiat, Rolls Royce and Nissan have
been flag-bearers for their respective countries.

By the 1990s, India had launched spacecraft and
missiles but it did not have a car that it could call its own—a
car that had been designed, developed and manufactured
within the country. Would India ever have a car worthy of
its national stature and pride?

Ratan Tata, who was at the time chairman of both
the Tata Group and Tata Motors, stood up in 1995 to
express his ambitions to manufacture an Indian car. He
issued a clarion call: 'We will have a car with the Zen's
size, the Ambassador's internal dimensions, the price of
a Maruti 800 and with the running cost of diesel.' Many
sceptics refused to believe an Indian car was possible
because the manufacture of cars requires the sort of
technology that India did not have at that time. But Ratan
Tata was determined. His team and he forged ahead with
a car project, the Tata Indica. Even this name spelt pride
for the nation.

Because a pioneering venture, by definition, means
going where no one has gone before, it inevitably has to
address many new challenges. The first of these, for the
Tata Indica, was world-class design. Skilled and passionate
engineers from the Engineering Research Centre of Tata
Motors in Pune undertook this exciting challenge, in
association with the Turin-based design house I.D.E.A.
The car had to be sleek and contemporary in its aesthetics,
but it also had to rise to Ratan Tata's clarion call of
providing enough space for an Indian family. It had to
withstand Indian roads, which were not amongst the best
in the world. The transmission system was also developed

entirely in-house, adding new capabilities to the company, which had no serious background in cars, having focused on commercial vehicles until then.

When the design for the Tata Indica was finally unveiled, the reactions were euphoric. Girish Wagh, who is now executive director at Tata Motors, was a young engineer in the company at that time. He says that when he first saw the Indica in the prototype shop of the factory, his first thought was, 'Wow, what a wonderful new Toyota car!' It was only when he got closer that he realized it was not another vehicle from the Japanese Zen master of cars but the new Tata car.

Everyone who saw the car fell in love with the design. It was distinctive, high on the coolness quotient and had international appeal. It was breakthrough global styling, but everything in it had been designed specifically for Indian roads and Indian families. India had never seen a car like this before.

The second challenge that Tata Motors had to address was the huge investment that would be required for a car manufacturing plant. A new plant would cost more than US$ 2 billion. Tata Motors could not afford this amount in those days. Would this make the project a non-starter? Once again, the pioneer in Ratan Tata said that something different had to be done. His team and he scoured the world for a more cost-effective alternative. They eventually found a disused Nissan plant in Australia, which they were able to purchase at one-fifth the cost of a new car manufacturing plant. The Tata Motors team disassembled this plant brick by brick, carried it across the seas and reassembled it in Pune. They accomplished this task within six months.

The third challenge ahead of Tata Motors was to develop indigenous components for the Tata Indica. The car had 3,885 discrete designed components, which had to be locally developed and manufactured, either by Tata Motors or by capable vendors. Many of these were being made for the first time in the country, and would require vendors to scale up their capabilities or even develop new skills. A special team called supplier quality improvement group (SQIG) was created for this purpose. Vendors had to be convinced to produce to the highest global standards, with very strict and narrow tolerances. For the manufacture of some specific components, joint ventures were formed with global giants, under a holding company called Tata AutoComp Systems.

More than 300 vendors were developed, creating a stream of 12,000 jobs. Eventually, nearly 98 per cent of all the parts used in the Indica were made in India, an amazing statistic for a country that had never before made its own car. It would be appropriate to say that this project gave birth to not just a new car but also to an entire new auto manufacturing ecosystem in the western region of India.

Then, operators had to be trained to assemble the car. Some of them still recall that it took them eight days to assemble the first Indica car. Today a new car emerges from the same factory in Pune every fifty-six seconds! These workers, to this day, are very proud that they were involved in the creation of the country's first indigenous car. They also recall that Ratan Tata was personally involved in leading the project, visiting their shop floors quite often throughout that period and even exchanging a few words with them. Here was a car that was manufactured not just with technological precision but also with great pride and love.

Having addressed all these challenges, the company eventually launched the Tata Indica in 1998 to fabulous bookings and consumer response. But it soon encountered several engineering and quality problems, such as uneven tyre wear, belt noise and defective pulleys, which led to significant criticism. Consumer complaints escalated and rival companies predicted the imminent death of the Indica. There is, of course, no dearth of condescending minds, both Western and Indian, which never miss an opportunity to take potshots at India and other nations of the global South.

In the midst of this intense backlash, Ratan Tata led from the front and steered the company's efforts towards bringing about the improvements which were immediately required. Within the team there was great resilience and a strong commitment to making this pioneering venture a great success. The team worked very hard, and it succeeded in resolving all the initial quality issues. A new, robust Indica was ready by 2001, with all the key quality problems addressed and completely eliminated. It was launched as the Tata Indica V2, with the advertising line 'Even more car per car'.

The Indica V2 made an immediate impact and was a brilliant success. It became the fastest-selling car in Indian history when it sold 1,00,000 units in less than eighteen months. Despite an overall economic slowdown in 2001, it recorded a handsome growth of over 46 per cent in that year. The reputed television program *BBC Wheels* declared the Indica as the 'best car in India in the Rs 3 lakh to Rs 5 lakh category'.

The team was ecstatic. The smiles were back. There had been a hiccup, but the team had proven itself more than capable. India's first indigenously designed car had proved to be a huge success. Today, in 2023, Tata Motors is a leading player in the space of passenger cars in India, the dominant market leader in electric vehicles . . . a proud Indian automobile brand. Behind all this was the pioneering spirit which had built the foundation for such sustained success at the Group.

Why did Ratan Tata take on the challenge of making India's own car? Listen to his own words:

> I had a strong conviction that our engineers, who could put a rocket into space, could produce our own car. And when we took up the challenge, we went out and got expertise wherever it was necessary. Everything we had in it was ours. So, to me, (the Indica) was a great feeling of national achievement.

This landmark project epitomizes the ability of the Group's leaders to take on a challenge, one that Ratan Tata has held out to himself and to the Tata Group at large: 'Can we do something that has never been done before?'

4

People

'No success or achievement in material terms is worthwhile unless it serves the needs or interests of the country and its people and is achieved by fair and honest means . . . good human relations not only bring great personal rewards but are essential to the success of any enterprise'—J.R.D. Tata's letter to K.C. Bhansali, a schoolteacher, 13 September 1965

This chapter is about people. The first story in this section narrates how Jamsetji Tata went about getting trusted and loyal managers to assist him in realizing his dreams. It would be obvious that for technical and experienced talent Jamsetji went abroad. However, for management and administration, which are rooted in local culture, he relied on Indians with sound experience of the country. Above all, he seemed to spend considerable personal time on what we would nowadays call 'human resources.' He did not delegate these tasks to an HR department, not just in the matter of managerial talent but also in the matter of factory labour and skilling. His personal interest in people resulted in his instituting dramatic measures (by the standards of those times) for labour welfare, training and social security.

The second of the stories narrates how, after fifty years, J.R.D. Tata did the same thing—assembling top-class professionals around himself, many of whom were far more skilled and qualified than him. His meticulous emphasis on skilling, talent pools, perfection and showcasing people management as the finest of arts is remarkable.

The third story is a first-hand account written by Harish about why he made the Tata Group his professional home for his entire career of thirty-six years and how the Group shaped him professionally. While this story is a personal perspective, it nonetheless highlights some important reasons why the Tata Group has been able to attract, retain and nurture talent over five generations.

We first explore the environment in which Jamsetji set out to build what must be considered among India's early large-scale enterprises. Here is a brief history of the factors that led to the establishment and growth of Indian management talent.

Growth of the Indian Manager

Circa 1800, India counted among the richest nations in the world in terms of GDP, which was why the Dutch, the English and the French, were all eager to trade with India. Recall what led to colonization. Textiles, spices, ivory and agricultural commodities were all hugely valuable trading items. The industrial revolution in England led to employment generation in mining, manufacturing, railways and the postal system, among many other areas. Apart from workers, the tribe of managers started to develop too. In their own interests, the British colonialists introduced infrastructure activities in their most prized colony. In the initial decades, experienced British workers and technicians worked in India as supervisors or managers. The activity reserved for the natives within India or other colonies in Africa, West Indies, Guyana or Fiji was that of unskilled labour.

Historians credit Dadabhai Naoroji with mooting and advocating the idea that 'natives' had to be trained and deployed to tackle the administrative challenges in a complex country like India. As a British Parliamentarian, Naoroji lobbied for the ICS cadre to admit suitable Indians. His mission met with initial success, when Indians were allowed to sit for the ICS exam. But the exam was conducted only in London. Naoroji then pushed for the ICS entrance exam to be held in India, concurrently with the exam in London. Several years later, ICS exams started to be held concurrently in Britain and India. It was in this manner that Indians were groomed to be ICS officers in India.

Meanwhile, railways and postal services started to be established in India. Progressively, Indians started to enter the defence forces as juniors. Private entrepreneurs took to modern industry, particularly in the domains of textiles, jute, coal, steel and tea. All such activities required administrative and management talent. Indians joined firms as junior staff members, and a few grew into junior managerial roles. This was largely true right into the 1930s, by which time Jamsetji's enterprises—textiles, steel, hydropower—were up and running.

International companies started to take deliberate steps to develop Indian management talent. Indian entrepreneurs started to develop their own ambitions. Textile mills came up in Bombay and Ahmedabad. Jute mills were set up in undivided Bengal. Tea plantations and factories were established in Assam, Kerala and Tamil Nadu. The Tatas set up a steel plant and hydroelectric power stations. All of them either recruited foreigners for technical help or trained their own manpower. These Indian entrepreneurs were focused on developing Indian managerial talent.

As can be seen from this brief review, talent building has been a complex and long journey, demanding great persistence and patience. Talent building represents the infinite game and has no quick-fix solutions.

People Are Tougher to Build than Factories

Efficient factories are daunting to build. First, there is land assessment, acquisition and preparation to be done. Then comes technology selection, equipment purchase, layout and installation. The third and toughest part consists of manpower planning, employee recruitment and, most importantly, skilling, training and motivating employees to deliver. Fourth comes the grand concertino of assembling the parts of the jigsaw before commissioning the factory. Finally comes the operation of the new plant on an optimum basis for efficiency and effectiveness. All this can take a decade, maybe more.

To build and sustain a company management cadre from the top leadership downwards is even more difficult and time-consuming. The talent process follows the rather imprecise art of judging how to develop human beings— from recruitment to evaluation, from creation of talent density to achievement of talent portability, from defining what a manager's responsibility is to holding the manager accountable and finally, to advancing the best talent out of a well-honed bench strength. These processes do not bear a direct cause-and-effect connection, unlike action and reaction in physics. Rather, the response occurs quite iteratively, to a series of events over long periods of time.

These events do not proceed linearly and often have unintended consequences. But such is the nature of the art of developing leadership, because it deals not with physical objects but with human beings.

The two toughest jobs in the world are perhaps parenting and building leadership talent for the long-term. Just as parenting cannot and should not be left to just one parent or to the grandparents, talent development cannot and must not be left exclusively to either the HR department or to the CEO. Talent development is a core responsibility of all leaders.

The distinguishing mark of a fine company is the glorious *jugalbandi* (duet) of its operations and human resources management.

A rigorous discipline of planning and pursuit of talent excellence is either weak or absent in many Indian companies. Quite often there exists no defined process. Where there is a semblance of process, it tends to be personality driven rather than process-driven. It is worthwhile for Indian corporations to work on this potential weak spot. Benchmarking processes against the best in class, just as management would do for total quality or productivity, is a good way forward. Too often, the chief executive officer leaves this complex task to personnel/HR, and deploys his or her personal energies on other equally important corporate issues. The comparing of talent management and parenting imaginatively highlights why excellence in talent management is among the toughest of corporate jobs.

Both require a rigorous and sustained process discipline soaked in a warm soup of empathy and emotion.

Shapers of Institutions

A few years ago, Gopal got involved in a piece of research on 'Shapers of Business Institutions'. Six companies participated in the research: L&T, HDFC, Kotak, Marico, TCS and Biocon. One question asked of the chief executive officers and leaders of these companies was about how much of their time went into 'reflecting, thinking and planning of management talent'. Their answers ranged from 25 per cent to 40 per cent.

Those numbers are astonishingly high, but they offer a clue as to how much top leaders value their own contribution to developing other leaders. When an individual becomes a top leader, one of his or her principal responsibilities is to develop other leaders for the organization.

The authors have experienced the ways in which talent management was nurtured in, for example, Tata Consultancy Services, Tata Steel and Titan. They are certainly impressed by the care and time leaders and HR bestow on nurturing and coaching talent within these companies. One measure of their success and capability is that, over several decades and leader successions, these companies can present more than one internal candidate to take over a vacancy so that it is filled without hesitation and without pause.

India is blessed to possess great leadership talent, but organizations must figure out how to cultivate and curate that talent.

To summarize our observations, for a long-standing corporation like the Tatas, it is essential to rely on distributed and professional leadership over generations of leaders. The Tatas have not been able to do this perfectly. But on the whole, with some exceptions, the Group has attracted and retained outstanding professionals over the decades, many of whom have been iconic in the Indian environment.

The first story in this chapter illustrates the approach of founder Jamsetji in the 1890s towards leadership and talent; the second story describes J.R.D. Tata's approach from the 1940s onwards and the last story by Harish Bhat is, if we may say so, a 'worm's eye view' of talent from a recruit's perspective.

Stories of People

1. Talent for a Start-up: Jamsetji Tata and His Remarkable Leadership Team

Jamsetji Tata is venerated as a visionary and a nation builder who conceived of India's first integrated steel plant, its first major hydroelectric power project and its first university of higher education in science. He is also known for his philosophy of putting the community at the centre of the enterprise he founded—the Tata Group, which began life as a small start-up.

However, what is not as well known is the thoughtful and often painstaking work he did in nurturing talent and building an outstanding yet diverse leadership team for his start-up enterprise. Without such talent by his side, he may never have got the Tata Group to develop wings to fly.

Take a quick look at the key members of Jamsetji's leadership team to see for yourself how different they were from each other in background and skill sets. There was Sir Bezonji Dadabhoy Mehta, who did not have any formal education and was an entirely self-made man. In sharp contrast to him stood Burjorji Padshah, a versatile genius with a brilliant academic record. Then there was R.D. Tata, Jamsetji's cousin, who had none of Burjorji's brilliance but knew finance well and was a very persistent man. Into this team, Jamsetji also successfully brought in a rank outsider, Charles Page Perin, one of the finest engineers of New York City. In addition to these names were Jamsetji's own sons, Dorabji and Ratanji.

Jamsetji assembled this start-up team himself. He was his own chief human resources officer (CHRO). In any case, the concept of the CHRO had not yet been born in those distant days. In each case, he looked for specific attributes and then took care to choose a man who possessed them. Thereafter, he provided his leaders with all the support they required, communicating extensively with them. Most importantly, he inspired them with the core purpose of his enterprise, which was building the community and nation.

How did he spot talent? Quite interestingly, he did this in many different ways. We must walk back in history and hear some of those stories.

In the case of Bezonji Mehta, the story commences when Jamsetji began looking for a factory manager for his first major greenfield project, the Empress Mills in Nagpur, which he founded in 1874. Jamsetji informed his friends that he was in search of a man who could help him manage this textile mill. He wanted a person who had common sense, honesty, intelligence and an open mind. He wanted a person whom he could train according to his own ideas.

Jamsetji heard about Bezonji through a colleague, Darashaw Chichgar. Bezonji was at that time a goods superintendent in the Great Indian Peninsula Railway.

He knew nothing about the cotton industry, but Jamsetji
was impressed with his organizational experience in the
railways. Very importantly, his qualities of character
appealed greatly to Jamsetji. It was based on this assessment
that Jamsetji Tata appointed Bezonji as manager of Empress
Mills, after two initial years of training.

Jamsetji worked closely with Bezonji during the first
few years, on challenges ranging from technology to labour.
Once these initial problems were addressed, Jamsetji
developed adequate comfort in Bezonji's leadership to
leave the development of Empress Mills entirely in his
care. Bezonji expanded the mills and made them even more
prosperous. He did this quite independently, and in doing
so, provided Jamsetji Tata the resources, space and time to
take forward his other big ideas such as steel, power and
the university for science.

Jamsetji not merely built an excellent rapport with
Bezonji but he also respected Bezonji's desire to continue
to live in Nagpur and manage Empress Mills. Bezonji even
refused an offer of a directorship in the parent company,
Tata Sons. Jamsetji was also generous in appreciating
Bezonji's contributions. Speaking at a meeting of the
company in Bombay in the later years of his life, Jamsetji
Tata said: 'That so vast a concern as this has grown to be
so successfully managed by a board of directors and a firm
of agents having their headquarters 500 miles away, is in
itself sufficient proof of Mr Bezonji's great merit.'

The story of how Burjorji Padshah was brought into
the Tata Group by Jamsetji is quite different. Jamsetji
knew Padshah since the time the latter was a child. After
Burjorji lost his father, Jamsetji became the guardian of

the family. Burjorji excelled in academics, graduating from Elphinstone College and later going on to study at Cambridge University. During his graduate studies, his versatile intellect was on full display—he won the Gibbs Prize in physics, the Ellis Scholarship in English, the James Taylor prize in history and economics and the Cobden medal in political economy.

After his education, Burjorji became a professor at Sindh College in Karachi, where he was very popular. However, he later resigned from this college on a matter of principle, when he was unfairly passed over for the principal's role, which went to an Englishman. Thereafter, he considered joining the Servants of India Society founded by Gopal Krishna Gokhale to serve the nation. This was the time when Jamsetji Tata stepped in, requesting Burjorji to join him in the Tata Group.

Jamsetji knew that Burjorji had a versatile intellect that could come in very useful in many areas. He also understood that the young man had a strong desire to contribute to the country. He suggested to Burjorji that he could render tremendous service to the nation by helping him with various important projects, starting with the initial exploration for establishing India's first university of higher education in science. This must have been a big attraction for Burjorji, since the world of academics and research had always appealed to his keen mind. And Jamsetji's timing was just right.

Burjorji agreed, and joined Jamsetji Tata as a key member of his leadership team. He immediately took on the investigations into the establishment of a research university, travelling to the USA and Europe to benchmark universities there and collect data relating to higher studies in science. His conclusions from this project led directly to the foundation of the Indian Institute of Science (IISc) in Bangalore.

Thereafter, Jamsetji requested Burjorji to support him in many other projects. For a very bright and versatile mind like his, this variety of work perhaps kept Burjorji fully engaged and happy. Jamsetji had therefore crafted a win-win solution for the man and for the group.

Later, after Jamsetji's demise, Burjorji also supported his son (and the second chairman of the Tata Group), Dorabji Tata in the same way. Burjorji was instrumental in crafting the success of Tata Steel and in helping establish the Tata hydroelectric power project. He also did all the research and study that went into the Tata Group's forays into banking, insurance and oil-based consumer products, such as soaps. Suffice it to say that he rendered invaluable services to the cause of India's industrialization—thanks to Jamsetji Tata having convinced him to join the Tatas and having nurtured his talent within the group.

Jamsetji's eye for outstanding talent also came to the fore in the case of his own cousin, R.D. Tata. R.D. (as he was called) worked in his father's independent trading firm based in Hong Kong. A few years after his father's demise in 1876, he took charge of the company, which was in a precarious state. With great financial acumen and persistence, he nursed it back to good health. Jamsetji Tata saw this and was impressed with R.D.'s financial capabilities. He decided to take him into Empress Mills and later made him a partner of the parent company, Tata and Sons, in 1887.

Jamsetji entrusted R.D. with running the trading and financial activities of the company. In later years, post

Jamsetji's passing away, R.D. steered the Tata Group through a very difficult period after the First World War. This was the period when many merchants had predicted the collapse of the Tata Group. R.D., with his maturity, persistence and financial expertise, ensured that the right actions were taken to bring the Tatas out of the woods.

A final story which illustrates Jamsetji Tata's focus on getting the right talent into his top team is that of Charles Page Perin, an eminent consulting engineer from New York City. Jamsetji's mind was set on bringing to India the technological expertise required for establishing the country's first integrated steel plant. He was then a relatively unknown Indian merchant. Yet, he travelled by ship to the USA, researched who the potential technical experts could be, zeroed in on the name of Charles Page Perin and then visited Perin's office in New York. There, he convinced Perin, one of the greatest engineers of the Western world, to leave the luxuries of New York and come to the jungles of eastern India to set up a steel plant here.

How did Jamsetji do this? Here is the story, as narrated by Charles Page Perin himself:

I was poring over some accounts in the office when the door opened, and a stranger in a strange garb entered. He walked in, leaned over my desk, and looked at me fully a minute in silence. Finally, he said in a deep voice, 'Are you Charles Page Perin?' I said, 'Yes'. He stared at me again silently for a long time. Then slowly he said, 'I believe I have found the man I have been looking for. Julian Kennedy has written to you that I am going to build a steel plant in India. I want you to come to India with me, to find suitable iron core and coking coal and the necessary fluxes. I want you to take charge as my consulting engineer. Mr. Kennedy will build the steel plant wherever you advise, and I will foot the bill. Will you come to India with me?

I was dumbfounded, naturally. But you don't know what character and force radiated from Tata's face. And kindliness, too. 'Well,' I said, 'yes, I will go.' And I did.

Charles Page Perin came to India and helped establish Tata Steel. What a fascinating story this is. Indeed, all the stories above—those of Bezonji Mehta, Burjorji Padshah, R.D. Tata and Charles Page Perin—are remarkable. Together they go to show how focused Jamsetji Tata was in spotting and building top-class leadership talent for the start-up that he had created.

2. J.R.D. Tata: A Leader of Leaders

J.R.D. Tata was an outstanding leader of men. During his tenure as its chairman, he built for the Tata Group the finest ensemble of corporate leadership that has ever existed in India. He had a sharp eye for spotting outstanding talent. He then set about attracting them to the Tata Group. Once they had joined, he empowered them to grow their own wings and fly. So many members of his leadership team were legends in their own right, yet JRD inspired them and earned their abiding respect and love.

Consider the galaxy of stars who worked with JRD across two generations. In the 1940s and 1950s, his

leadership team at Tata Sons consisted of towering
stalwarts such as Sir Homi Mody, A.D. Shroff, Dr John
Mathai, Ardershir Dalal and Naval Tata. After the 1960s,
a second generation of equally accomplished leaders sat
on the board of Tata Sons and constituted JRD's core
team. They included the likes of Sumant Moolgaokar,
Darbari Seth, Nani Palkhivala, Rusi Mody, J.J. Bhabha
and Ratan Tata.

JRD led these accomplished people on the strength
of his principles, by empowering them and by building
consensus where it was required. Most importantly, he
inspired these accomplished leaders to stretch beyond
themselves and often achieve the impossible. Speaking of
how he did this, JRD himself once revealed his secret sauce
of leadership: 'If I have any merit, it is getting along with
individuals, according to their ways and characteristics.
At times, it involves suppressing yourself. It is painful,
but necessary. To be a leader you have got to lead human
beings with affection.'

At the heart of J.R.D. Tata's ability to build and nurture
a strong team was his eye for spotting exceptional talent
for specific roles. He would then convince them to join
the group. Without such highly talented individuals at his
side, JRD's leadership would perhaps not have flowered as
beautifully as it did.

Consider the story of Sumant Moolgaokar, the man
who went on to build a veritable powerhouse, Tata
Motors. During the 1940s, J.R.D. Tata had been on a
learning mission to visit industries in the UK and the USA.
Accompanying him on this visit was a young Moolgaokar,
forty years old, at that time a director of the Associated

Cement Companies (ACC). During this visit, JRD saw how passionate this young man was about engineering and factories. He had already known about Moolgaokar's brilliance in creating India's first cement plant. JRD felt increasingly certain that this was the man to lead a new project that the Tatas were about to launch, the Tata Engineering and Locomotive Company (TELCO, which has since been renamed as Tata Motors).

When they were back in India, JRD asked him, 'How long are you going to make the glue that sticks the bricks together?' He then approached the chairman of ACC, Sir Homi Mody, with a request that he release Moolgaokar to TELCO. JRD's request was initially refused, because Sir Homi felt that ACC required the man. But JRD persisted. He approached Sir Homi Mody once again. Eventually, Sir Homi agreed. How long could he keep saying no to the chairman of the Tata Group!

JRD then brought Sumant Moolgaokar on board as director-in-charge of TELCO. This was in 1949, when Moolgaokar was only forty-three years old, much below the age associated with directorship in those days (and perhaps even today). This is testimony to the belief JRD had in people once he had identified the right leaders.

For the next four decades, in most matters relating to TELCO, JRD deferred to Sumant Moolgaokar's expertise and judgement even while providing guidance where required. He did this because he quickly understood Moolgaokar's style of leadership. Many years later, JRD revealed this to his biographer R.M. Lala: 'I realized early that Sumant was a lone wolf. If I let him run it his way he would deliver the goods. And he did.'

JRD was, however, a constant source of motivation and support, which kept Moolgaokar's spirits high even during challenging times, and encouraged him to deliver his best. For instance, in 1974, when Moolgaokar completed twenty-five years with the Tatas, JRD wrote him a wonderful letter, which remains a benchmark in motivational communication. In this letter, JRD tells him: 'As I think of what you have achieved during this quarter of a century, I feel that if the only thing I had done for Tatas was to inveigle you into the firm, I would have earned my salary for the whole of my career with them.'

Can you imagine receiving such a letter from the chairman of your company?

The story of Nani Palkhivala, yet another outstanding leader in J.R.D. Tata's top team, is similar yet different, and highlights JRD's adaptability when it came to bringing on board exceptional talent. JRD learnt about the legal brilliance of Nani Palkhivala through one of the then senior directors of the Tata Group, A.D. Shroff. Nani was around forty years of age at that time and a rising star in the firmament of taxation law. JRD was determined to bring him on board because he saw the enormous value that Nani could add in the future to the group.

It is said that legal luminaries such as Justice Yeshwant Chandrachud attempted to dissuade Nani Palkhivala from joining the Tata Group so that he could continue his promising career as a lawyer, unfettered by any corporate pressures. JRD quickly grasped that Nani was very keen to work as an independent lawyer. So he offered Nani Palkhivala a directorship in the Tata Group, while allowing him to also continue his independent legal practice. JRD was also able to convince Nani that by being part of the leadership team of the Tata Group he would be able to serve society better than if he were only a lawyer.

Nani Palkhivala joined the Tata Group in April 1961 and continued to serve the Group as its legal head and director with distinction for the next three decades. He continued his own legal practice throughout this period, and JRD stayed true to his commitment of permitting him the independence to do this, including his involvement in a sensitive legal case involving the then prime minister, Indira Gandhi. Truly speaking, JRD had crafted a win-win relationship between the Tata Group and one of the finest intellects of independent India.

A third story illustrates how J.R.D. Tata spotted extraordinary talent from within the group, providing highly capable employees a platform to make a big impact. In 1939, under JRD's leadership, Tata Chemicals had been created. It came up in the arid Okhamandal region of Gujarat, where an earlier enterprise called the Okha Salt Works had collapsed. The Tatas had taken over this company because JRD felt that there was a real opportunity to pioneer an inorganic chemicals industry in the country, manufacturing soda ash and other related products.

However, soda ash manufacture was a closely guarded secret, and consultants began advising JRD to exit the industry. They said the location was not right and the business was destined for failure. The Tata Group was about to engage the services of a foreign firm to help, when J.R.D. Tata, at a review meeting, met a young chemical engineer called Darbari Seth. Seth debunked the proposal of the foreign firm and presented with enthusiasm his dream idea for the manufacture of soda ash at Tata Chemicals and the details of how he would go about making this happen.

His enthusiasm was infectious, and JRD could feel the spark in this young man, though he could not understand all the technical details that Seth was putting forward. Back in his office, JRD studied Seth's background and found that the youngster was very well qualified. He had worked in Dow Chemicals in the USA and had also earlier designed a soda ash plant in Holland. However, at Tata Chemicals, Seth was still in a relatively junior role and his managers were unwilling to listen to his ideas.

J.R.D. Tata reflected on his interaction with Seth, and on these details. He came to the considered conclusion that Darbari Seth, with his deep expertise, unbridled enthusiasm and lateral thinking, could make Tata Chemicals a success. Immediately, he instructed the management to put Seth in charge of the soda ash plant, notwithstanding his youth. And he provided Seth all the support required as he navigated uncharted waters.

Darbari Seth went on to develop and implement the technology required, and he made Tata Chemicals a huge success, navigating many challenging situations over the years. He led the company until his retirement in the 1990s and was recognized across the country as a technocrat par excellence. In addition, he led the Tata Group's foray into a few other industries too, including tea and coffee. Once again, JRD's eye for talent had delivered results.

Even as JRD observed with satisfaction the results being delivered by Moolgaokar, Palkhivala, Seth and other members he had brought into his leadership team, he was also keen to institutionalize the onboarding of exceptional talent into the Tata Group so that a pipeline of leadership could be created for a sustainable future. To ensure this, he created the Tata Administrative Service (TAS) in 1956 as a flagship leadership programme. This was the first such programme in corporate India.

Over the years, several TAS officers have gone on to lead companies of the Group with distinction. Some of them have also been pioneers, creating new companies or undertaking path-breaking acquisitions. Two standout names from the early years of the TAS are worth mentioning here: Xerxes Desai, the man who created Titan, India's most successful lifestyle company and R.K. Krishna Kumar, the leader who built Tata Tea and led the acquisition of Tetley, the first ever foreign brand to be bought by an Indian company. JRD inspired both.

J.R.D. Tata's abiding focus on talent not only enhanced the Tata Group but also totally transformed its fortunes. Like King Arthur and his brave knights of the round table, JRD and his band of exceptional leaders will be talked about for a very long time.

3. How the Tata Group Became My Professional Home

(A personal essay by Harish Bhat)

So many people have asked me, 'Why have you spent your entire career, nearly four decades now, with the Tata Group? Is this not unusual in today's day and age?' I respond to them with, 'It's not just me, tens of thousands of my colleagues stay and work in this group for their entire careers. We see this not just as a job but as our professional home. Why would we leave our homes unless there is a strong reason to?'

They are keen to pursue the conversation. In a world where people change jobs every few years, how does the Tata Group retain talent for such long periods of time? What is the secret to the group building such a strong pipeline of talent in many of its companies?

Rather than provide a conceptual response, let me attempt to answer this question here by narrating my own story. Many of my senior colleagues in the group would have similar stories of their own, which may differ in their details but whose broad arc would perhaps be the same.

I joined the Tata Group as an officer in the Tata Administrative Service (TAS) in 1987. At the point of my graduation from business school (IIMA), I attended the TAS selection interviews that were held in Ahmedabad. I did this because some of my seniors in college, and one of my professors, had told me that the Tata Group was a pretty good place to work in and conducted its business on sound principles. I had also heard of J.R.D. Tata, then the chairman of the group, and regarded him with awe. Beyond that I knew little about the Tatas; neither did I know anyone of influence within the group.

I was shortlisted for the final interviews, which were held at the headquarters of the group, Bombay House. The Tatas also gave me an air ticket to travel from Ahmedabad to Mumbai. This was my first ever flight as an adult, and as the flight descended in Mumbai, I looked out of the windows at this vast city and wondered what lay ahead of me.

For my final interview, I was called into the grand and formidable boardroom on the fourth floor of Bombay House. The eight-member interview panel included luminaries like Ratan Tata, J.J. Bhabha and R.K. Krishna Kumar. That afternoon we had an opportunity to briefly meet J.R.D. Tata himself. I was amazed that the Tata Group would take such efforts to recruit freshers like us. I thought to myself, this says something about the group. Later that evening, I was delighted when I was informed that I had been selected for TAS.

During the first month of my life with the Tatas, my TAS batch mates and I had the opportunity to meet and interact with legends like Russi Mody, Jamshed Irani, Darbari Seth, Noshir Soonawala, Sumant Moolgaokar and Xerxes Desai. Each of them spent considerable time with us. For instance, Russi Mody flew us himself from Jamshedpur to the mines in Noamundi, and spoke to us for several hours on a wide range of subjects. All this was such a fabulous start.

Over the next several years the Tata Group gave me many wonderful platforms to learn, contribute and grow. I began as executive assistant to the managing director of Tata Tea, R.K. Krishna Kumar (also known as KK to his friends and colleagues). From him I learnt not just the sanctity of hard work and delivering results, but also the importance of kindness and compassion. Then I also served as project manager in the office of the chairman of the company, Darbari Seth. This was an opportunity of a lifetime. Every day in his office was worth a full MBA programme. Both these senior leaders were generous with their time and guidance. These stints provided me with exposure to decision-making at the highest levels of an organization, and also to what strong, value-focused leadership really meant on a day-to-day basis. In providing me these invaluable experiences right at the start of my career, the Tata Group helped me build a strong foundation for my corporate voyage ahead.

Thereafter, I was given the invaluable opportunity to lead a sales and marketing team at Tata Tea. We were a small company then, with little or no market share in the packaged tea market, and we were competing with a giant, Hindustan Unilever, which was the dominant market leader. I was empowered to take the bold decisions required to shape the markets I led, and was permitted to make mistakes too, provided my intent was right. We launched new brands, created new campaigns, and put together and nurtured a new distribution network. This was exciting and heady work, and it gave me superb exposure to the nuts and bolts of marketing. I also learnt a thing or two about how to face and outpace fierce competition in the field. We worked hard and smart, and kept gaining market share year after year until Tata Tea eventually became a leader in many markets. I could not have asked for a better start to my sales and marketing career.

The three decades that followed were a blend of fabulous experiences that I relished totally, even as I learnt from them. I was provided an opportunity to be part of the core team that engineered the acquisition of Tetley, the first global brand to be bought by an Indian company. This assignment gave me an excellent albeit brief exposure to the global markets and to the process of mergers and acquisitions.

Thereafter, even as I was doing very well in the tea business, the Tata Group moved me out of this zone of comfort to the jewellery business of Titan, which had made losses for several initial years since its establishment. I accepted this move as a professional challenge, and it was perhaps the defining stint of my career. I was part of a small leadership team that crafted the turnaround of Tanishq and laid the foundation for its future growth.

Then came a brief assignment in the telecom business in the Group, where success was difficult to come by, but I came away with some important learnings from this role. Thereafter, I had a much longer stint as the chief operating officer of the watches and wearables business of Titan, helping build great businesses around brands such as Titan, Fastrack and Sonata—all catering to different segments of the market. These leadership roles taught me the art and science of driving profitable growth, and of successfully leading large teams. I continued to learn from iconic leaders whom I had the opportunity to work with, such as Xerxes Desai, Jacob Kurian and Bhaskar Bhat.

By this time I had also got a ringside view of how the Tata Group kept the community centre stage at all times—whether the plantation workers in the tea estates, the karigars (artisans) who made jewellery or by creating a new flagship cancer hospital at Kolkata. I was inspired enough to want to write a book on the group and sought a sabbatical for this purpose. This was perhaps an unusual request from a COO of a business, but nonetheless it was given due consideration. Bhaskar Bhat, managing director of Titan, after consulting the Tata Group headquarters, permitted me to take a six-month sabbatical to research and write this book. Not just that, R. Gopalakrishnan, executive director at Tata Sons and a reputed author himself, actively mentored me in the writing of this book. For me this was a dream come true. Where else would I have found such a nurturing environment? *Tata Log*, my first book, was published at the end of 2012, and it went on to become a national bestseller. It also set me on a beautiful new voyage to become an author, alongside my career as a corporate manager.

When I returned from my sabbatical, I was offered the position of managing director and CEO of the company where I had begun my career twenty-five years ago, Tata Global Beverages (as Tata Tea was called by then). Soon after, the chairman of the Tata Group at that time, Cyrus Mistry, was keen that I serve as a member of the group executive council at Tata Sons. I played this role to the best of my ability, and also served as a non-executive director on the boards of some Tata companies, primarily in the consumer and retail sector, which I had got to know well.

In my last full-time role with the Tata Group, I served as brand custodian, leading the initiatives of India's most valuable brand, Tata, and working closely with the chairman of the Group, N. Chandrasekaran. Here again, I was given the opportunity to nurture and shape an iconic brand, which I did to the best of my capability, with a lot of love and care, until I retired from this role after my superannuation at the end of 2023.

Leading and managing a brand like Tata, which is a national asset and is used by so many companies of the group, is a complex task that requires clarity, balance, maturity and agility. During my final two years in this role,

Forbes listed me as amongst the top ten chief marketing officers in the world. I was proud to bring home this honour to the Tata Group and to India. In many ways, this global recognition was a tribute to how well the Tata Group had nurtured me over the past thirty-six years, ever since I walked in for that interview in Bombay House in 1987 as a young man of twenty-four.

During these thirty-six rewarding years, not once was I asked to do anything that went against my conscience. This is a tribute to the sound principles and ethical business practices that are at the heart of the Tata Group. This also meant that I could sleep well at night for all these years, which is worth its weight in gold.

I also felt immensely proud that I was part of a group whose core mission was nation-building. Owned by the Tata Charitable Trusts and driven by the founder's vision of keeping the community centre stage, this mission gave me a unique purpose for all that I was doing. By working in the Tata Group, I was indeed earning my livelihood, working in very interesting roles across sectors, learning from legendary leaders, progressing in my career quite steadily and making an impact in the industries I was part of. All that, yes. But, most importantly, I was also contributing to the nation.

This is my story. It is perhaps also the story of many of my colleagues in the Tata Group, though their individual details may differ. It is the story of why so many competent professionals choose to stay with the Tata Group for years together, and often for their entire working lives.

5

Progress

'After the initial period of basking in the glory . . . I settled down to figure out what was required . . . broadly we agreed that the group should be restructured to become more competitive, to provide better returns to shareholders, to be more nimble-footed or more proactive to the changing scene'—Ratan N. Tata, in his epilogue to R.M. Lala's book *The Creation of Wealth*

An institution that has survived for over a century, as the Tata Group has, must have certainly adapted to the changing times, technologies and markets. The progress of the institution depends on its having made strategic choices as to what it will do, and what it will not do.

There are three stories that accompany this essay. The first is about how Jamsetji set up a shipping line. The second is about how the Tatas set up an information technology company (then called data processing), Tata Consultancy Services (TCS). And the last is about how the Tatas morphed from being almost wholly a successful business-to-business group to becoming partly a business-to-consumer conglomerate.

It is instructive to recount how the Tata Group has morphed over its lifetime.

If our grandfathers were alive, they would think of the Tata Group as a textile concern, which is what the Tatas were around the 1880s. Despite the stunning success of his textiles business, Jamsetji seemed to have developed an infatuation with two industries of the future—steel and hydroelectric power.

Our fathers thought of the Tata Group as a steel and electricity company, which were the predominant areas of activity of the group in the first half of the 1900s. By the time the authors of this book became adults, the Tata Group was also seen as a truck manufacturer, apart from steel and electricity producer, making initial stirrings in software and consumer products.

It is not that new lines of business were added relentlessly without making space for them. The group also exited old lines of business, like textiles, cement, soaps and detergents, which no longer fitted with the priorities that the group saw for itself. The portfolio changes within the group illustrated the principle of 'creative destruction'.

One striking feature of all Tata Group projects is their inclusion, always, of some sort of social purpose. Jamsetji felt the hydroelectric project could help to make Mumbai a 'smokeless city'. Setting up hospitals and green patches in and around the company's factories ensured that his welfare measures were generous and well ahead of the times. Jamsetji is reported to have disliked 'patchwork philanthropy' and backed 'constructive philanthropy'.

What IBM founder Thomas J. Watson is reported to have told his executives in 1926 of his own company may be pertinent here (separately, IBM had partnered with the Tatas in the 1990s):

> This business of ours has a future. It has a past of which we are all proud, but it has a future that will extend beyond your lifetime and mine. This business has a future for your sons and grandsons, because it is going on forever. IBM is not merely an organization of men; it is an institution that will go on forever.[1]

Although Jamsetji did not make such a statement, his behaviour and actions reflected a similar spirit. Whenever Jamsetji entered a new business, he ran it as though it would run for the long term. Making a quick buck through short-term measures did not much appeal to him. This is perhaps the reason why some of the oldest companies on the Indian stock exchange are from the Tata stable: Indian Hotels Company (owner of the Taj brand), Tata Steel, Tata Power . . . all date back to the period before the First World War!

When a business idea did not work out, despite trying all alternatives to revive it, Jamsetji was quite open to shutting it down—as happened with the shipping line. This is another hallmark of the Tata Group. In more recent times, Tata's entry into the consumer telecom business did not work out, and after trying everything possible the group cut its losses and exited the industry. Perhaps this is an attribute of other great leaders too.

Andrew Carnegie, for example, was more or less a contemporary of Jamsetji's, but on the other side of the Atlantic. There is no evidence that Carnegie and Jamsetji ever met, even though they had a shared passion for steel. We know that they both attended the World Fair in America in 1893, but there is no evidence that they ever met.

Jamsetji had heard Thomas Carlyle in London saying something to the effect that the nation that has steel will own gold. By 1872, Carnegie had become convinced that steel would lie at the centre of the world of real work and set up his fledgling iron and steel enterprise. Thus, Carnegie and Jamsetji Tata set out on a somewhat similar quest, sequentially.

The important point about these leaders is that their success owes not only to the good decisions they made but also to the bad decisions they avoided. Take two examples: the rupture of the relationship between Andrew Carnegie and his mentor Tom Scott, and that between Thomas Watson with his mentor John Patterson.

Carnegie and his good senior friend and mentor Tom Scott shared deep emotional ties. Tom Scott set up a railroad company, Texas and Pacific, but financed it with too many short-term loans. Carnegie advised him against the venture. Sure enough, this situation led to financial trouble for Scott, and by 1873 a meeting of his friends and well-wishers was convened to help Scott out of the situation. Most of those who attended were prepared to help Scott, but Carnegie declined. Carnegie writes about it in his autobiography: 'I was then asked if I would bring them all to ruin by refusing to stand by my friends . . . The question of what was my duty came first and prevented that . . . it was one of the most trying moments of my whole life.' His refusal to help a dear friend must have been a trying experience, but Carnegie felt quite strongly that he needed every dollar he had for his own steel venture. Carnegie made a strategic choice, and painful though it was, he conserved his dollars for his own venture rather than propping up his friend's venture. This illustrates how choices have to be made in business—tough choices, but without emotional baggage.

Another such example can be drawn from the life of Thomas Watson, the founder of IBM. John Henry Patterson was the mentor who had groomed the young Tom Watson. Patterson was the super salesperson who

influenced Watson to make superior salesmanship a
primary strategic tool. Patterson had bought the National
Cash Register Company (NCR) in 1884, and Watson was
personally groomed into a senior management role by
Patterson. Patterson was one of those great paradoxes of
American entrepreneurship—a combination of rock-solid
personal honesty but practising base corporate corruption,
both marching hand in hand. This unholy combination
landed NCR in the clutches of the authorities, which led to
the indictment of the top people, including Watson. This
incident, and another, led to a permanent rupture in the
Patterson-Watson relationship. Watson then set out to join
Computing, Tabulating, Recording (CTR) Company, the
Neanderthal version of what became IBM later.

In some ways, a reader going through the biography of
Thomas Watson may note a vague resemblance between him
and Jamsetji Tata. Both were highly interested in embracing
the future. In fact, Watson established in 1929 a brand-new
department called the Future Demands Department. The
mandate of this department was 'to lead the way towards
creation and development of new products to cover new
fields'.[2] He may not have known that the Great Depression
was around the corner, yet deep into the Depression Watson
set up a new research and engineering laboratory because,
as he said, 'the future of our business largely depends on the
efforts, brains, and ability of our engineering department.'[3]

* * *

Let us return from these comparisons with contemporaries
to our three narratives relating to Tata and strategy. The Tata

Shipping Line was Jamsetji's response to the monopolistic practices of the dominant shipping line, Peninsular and Oriental (P & O). It could not survive so it was shut down in a few years. Interestingly, the Swadeshi Steamship Navigation Company (SSNC) was set up some years later, in 1906, by V.O. Chidambaram Pillai, popularly called VOC, a nationalist, to compete against the monopoly of the British India Steam Navigation Company. VOC was a legal pleader from Tuticorin, who promoted the company as a nationalist and a freedom fighter. On sober reflection, we wonder if Jamsetji cannot also be given the sobriquet of being 'a nationalist and a freedom fighter'.

The second narrative pertains to the entry of the Tata Group into information technology services through Tata Consultancy Services (TCS). Faqir Chand Kohli, the doughty founder of TCS, gave up a promising academic and research career in America to help his family, which had suffered the ravages of Partition in India. This story too has a tinge of nationalism. However, one of its foremost features is a consistent focus on sound strategy and disciplined growth.

The third narrative illustrates the systematic entry of the Tata Group into branded consumer businesses in the modern age. The only early successful entry of the group in this area had been through the pioneering entry of Taj Hotels. Its presence in the consumer vertical was strengthened in the 1980s and beyond through the wrist watches company Titan, by introducing branding in an unorganized industry like jewellery through Tanishq, by creating a fast-moving consumer products entity marketing tea, coffee, salt and spices, and by establishing itself in the

The four partners (clockwise from left): Jamsetji N. Tata, founder of the Tata Group; R.D. Tata, father of J.R.D. Tata; Ratan Tata, the younger son of the founder; and Dorab Tata, the elder son.

Dorabji Tata, second chairman of the Tata Group. He made many of Jamsetji Tata's dream projects come alive. When Tata Steel was passing through a difficult phase in 1924, his wife, Meherbai, and he pledged their entire personal wealth to save the company from its collapse.

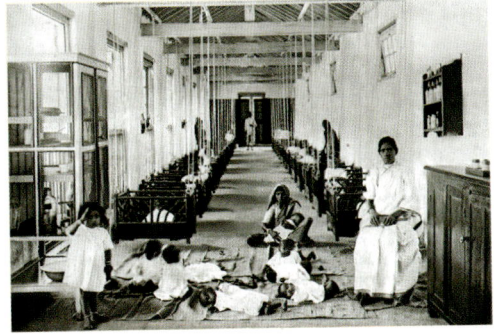

The creche at Empress Mills, circa 1919. Empress Mills in Nagpur was the first greenfield industrial enterprise of the Tata Group. It was also where Jamsetji Tata introduced many pioneering measures for the welfare of workers.

J.R.D. Tata, the chairman of the Tata Group for over fifty years was also the founder of Tata Airlines, which later went on to become Air India.

Ratan N. Tata, the fifth chairman of the Tata Group, drives the first Tata Indica off the assembly line at the Tata Motors plant in Pune in 1998.

Tata Memorial Hospital at Parel in Mumbai. Inaugurated in 1941, it is India's first cancer care hospital.

Indian Institute of Science, Bangalore. India's first university of higher education in science, which took birth because of the vision and persistence of Jamsetji Tata.

Darbari Seth, the man who led Tata Chemicals successfully through many challenges. He was a key member of J.R.D. Tata's leadership team.

F.C. Kohli, co-founder and first CEO of Tata Consultancy Services. He is referred to as the 'father of the Indian I.T. industry'. He was a key member of J.R.D. Tata's leadership team.

An early pack of Tata Tea, which transformed the branded tea market in India. Positioned on the platform of 'Asli Taazgi' (real freshness), this brand soon became a household favourite across India.

emerging field of 'organized retailing' through its Westside, Zudio and Croma stores, as well as other offerings.

These are great examples of progress through strategic choices made over several decades.

Stories of Progress

1. The Tata Shipping Line

Jamsetji Tata, founder of the Tata Group, is well known for establishing very successful pioneering business ventures, including Empress Mills, Svadeshi Mills, Ahmedabad Advance Mills, Tata Steel and Tata Power. These businesses not merely delivered excellent commercial returns but also helped shape modern Indian industry. This success is testimony to Jamsetji's strategic acumen, because in each of these ventures, he saw great business opportunity and also carved out a path to create sustained value.

However, did you know that not all of Jamsetji's dreams and business ventures succeeded? Some of them did not come to fruition, often because Jamsetji was not fully convinced of the feasibility of the business. In other cases, where a venture had been launched but he did not see a path to success despite persistent efforts at it, he took timely, strategic calls to exit the business. These were tough calls to make for a successful businessman of high standing. However, Jamsetji believed that good strategy

116

was all about making the right choices, notwithstanding how difficult those decisions were. One place where he had to make such a hard choice was in the case of the Tata Shipping Line.

The pre-eminent shipping line that carried exports from India during those days (1880s and 1890s) was the English P.&O., which had the support of the British Indian government. P&O had a virtual monopoly on shipping from India, and it soon began charging Indian merchants exorbitant freight rates. On the other hand, it provided greater rebates to British and Jewish firms, thus creating an uneven playing field for Indians. Jamsetji Tata, who was in the textiles business at that time, was adversely impacted, and he felt that this was very unfair to Indians.

So Jamsetji travelled to Japan, with the objective of striking up a collaboration with Nippon Yusen Kaisha (NYK), which was the largest shipping line of that country. He met the directors of NYK there. They agreed to partner with Jamsetji provided he took an equal risk in the venture and ran the ships on his own.

Having obtained this agreement with NYK, Jamsetji took forward this project with determination. To begin with, he chartered an English ship, called the *Annie Barrow*, at a fixed rate of £1,050 per month. He made this the first vessel of his new shipping company, which he called the 'Tata Line'. In fact, this was the first ever business of the Tata Group which bore the Tata name. Jamsetji wrote to his sons: 'I suggest that it be called the Tata Line so that it may serve as an incentive to our family to make it a permanent one, as far as it may be in our power.' That power would, however, be put to the test very soon.

Jamsetji felt that this venture would benefit not only his own textile business but also the entire Indian textile industry, which could now break free of the P.&O. monopoly and obtain lower shipping rates. A second ship, the *Lindisfarne*, was also chartered soon. NYK also loaned two vessels to this venture. Critical to the success of this venture was the full utilization of all these ships, which required a minimum quantity of freight, sourced both from Jamsetji Tata's own textile mills and also the factories belonging to other Indian merchants.

Indian media cheered Jamsetji's Tata Line and his daring effort to break a monopoly. The *Tribune* newspaper, writing in October 1894, said this effort had 'been the subject of general praise in the industrial centre of India'. The Tata Line determined to charge fair rates, since the very purpose of the venture was to ensure that Indian merchants got access to competitive shipping prices.

With this in mind, the Tata Line began charging Rs 12 per ton of freight, which was considered a fair and competitive price, compared to the very high rate of Rs 19 per ton being charged by P.&O., which had thus far enjoyed a monopoly. P.&O. reacted immediately, announcing that it would reduce rates dramatically, to Rs 1.8 per ton. However, merchants could only obtain this rate if they signed an agreement with P.&O. that they would not use the Tata Line or ships belonging to NYK. In addition, for specific merchants, P.&O. also offered to carry their cotton to Japan free of charge.

In addition to this 'war of freights', P.&O. also began to disparage the Tata Line, spreading word that one of the Tata ships, the *Lindisfarne*, was unfit to carry cotton (this was a wrong allegation that was also conveyed to the insurance agents. It was later dismissed by the agents after Jamsetji made his case to them). Clearly, through these drastic measures, P.&O. was trying to protect its monopoly and ensure that no Indian shipper began using the Tata Line.

Jamsetji Tata took up this matter strongly with the British government of India. He wrote to the Secretary of State for India and also published a pamphlet titled 'The War of Freights'. In this pamphlet, he made the point that P.&O.'s actions were motivated by their desire to destroy a possible rival in order to preserve their 'inordinate gains'. Therefore, they had driven freight down to an 'unremunerative and ruinous level' so that their rivals, including the Tata Line, were driven away. Once this happened, they would raise the rates once again, perhaps even higher than before.

In his letter to the Secretary of State, Jamsetji made the point that the P.&O. line, which had the support of the British government of India, was subsidized by taxpayers in India. That was how they could afford to engage in this unfair war of freights. Jamsetji wrote:

> This Company, to whose prosperity the taxpayers of India may lay some claim to have contributed, has driven off all legitimate competition from time to time, either by reducing rates to so low a limit as to exhaust the resources of its rivals . . . Indian shippers have been forced to endure this tyranny.

Jamsetji also protested against the P.&O. line giving rebates only to certain select, non-Indian firms.

The British government kept silent and took no action on Jamsetji's complaint, despite his persistent efforts. It appeared that their clear motive was to support the P.&O. line. Gradually, Indian merchants withdrew from the contracts they had entered into with the Tata Line because they were getting far lower rates from P.&O. They did not heed Jamsetji's appeals that it was essential to have an Indian shipping line competing with P.&O. to protect their long-term interests. They also did not listen to his warnings that if the Tata Line closed down, P.&O. would raise rates steeply once again.

Also, anonymous letters were published in the local newspapers questioning Jamsetji Tata's patriotic motives in starting the Tata Line. These letters went on to say that Jamsetji was acting totally for his own monetary gains. The only set of people who continued to send their freights on the Tata Line were the Japanese Cotton Buyer's Association, who kept to the letter and spirit of their contracts.

But this was not enough, and utilization of Jamsetji's ships fell dramatically, making their continued plying of the seas unremunerative. It was also clear that the government was unwilling to take any action to stop P.&O.'s unfair practices. Jamsetji was deeply distressed, but he thought through the situation deeply. He had already spent over one lakh rupees on the Tata Line. Each month, this business was costing him losses running up to tens of thousands of rupees. These were very large amounts in the 1890s.

At the end of this strategic reflection, he appears to have reached the conclusion that there was no sustainable or feasible way forward for the Tata Line. He then decided, quite clinically, to shut down this business, notwithstanding the risks that this closure could pose for his reputation as a very successful entrepreneur. He sent back to England the ships he had leased, and the Tata Line was, sadly, shut down.

Most of Jamsetji Tata's ventures succeeded brilliantly. The Tata Line is one that did not. The story of this venture, Jamsetji's initial vision as well as his decision to exit from it when he saw no ray of hope, as the industry was dominated by an unfair monopoly strongly supported by the then government, tells us that he did not shy away from making the right strategic choices untainted by emotion.

2. The Consistent and Disciplined Growth of TCS

This story is an account of how TCS was born, the strategic choices its leaders made in the early years, and how the organization has consistently grown from strength to strength.

One could say with hindsight that the darkest period of the licence-permit raj in India was from 1965 to 1980. One needed a license, to produce anything or to import equipment to produce anything. To sell what was produced, very often one's pricing required government permission. Government clearances were required if, through increased efficiency, more goods were produced using the same equipment.

It was in this constrictive time that the house of Tata first set up a separate computing division. The proposal was taken to J.R.D. Tata by Colonel Leslie Sawhney, a director at the Tatas and JRD's sister's husband. His idea was to centralize the data processing for the Tata companies' voluminous paperwork. The activity was housed as a division within Tata Sons, and in course of time came to be called TCS.

There were hardly any computers in India at that time, at best some International Business Machines (IBM) and International Computers Limited (ICL) machines. Some of the early executives at TCS in those times were Lalit Kanodia, Nitin Patel and Ashok Malhotra, all alumni of MIT.

Their initial groundwork and experimentation took recognizable shape when Faqir Chand Kohli joined the effort. The formation of TCS is yet another example of the group entering the latest and emerging fields as a conscious strategy. Kohli was a power engineer, also from MIT— Tata's ability to attract the best talent seems relevant to highlight here again.

Kohli was the son of a textile merchant in Peshawar. After completing his BA (Honors) in English from Lahore in undivided India, he acquired an additional degree in applied mathematics and physics. Being a bright student, he then secured a government scholarship to study in Canada. He graduated as an electrical engineer from Kingston, Ontario, and went on to secure a tuition-free master's degree from MIT.

With such an impressive background, he could have been tempted to stay and work abroad, but the appalling condition of his family in Lucknow after the ravages of Partition moved him so intensely that he sought a job in India. Kohli received an offer from Tata Electric Company (TEC) in 1951. He was a fabulous asset to Tata Electric. By 1965, Kohli had steered Tata Electric into becoming the third company *in the world* to employ a digital computer to plan power load dispatches. Kohli's boss, Dr P.M. Agarwala, the then managing director of Tata Electric, took note of the intellectual acumen and computer knowledge that Kohli had acquired. TCS had been set up within Tata Sons. Agarwala persuaded Kohli to take up the leadership of TCS. For a star in a big Tata Company to accept the leadership of a small, unknown division of Tata Sons was not natural. It is to the credit of Agarwala's persuasive skills and Kohli's entrepreneurship that he did take up the challenge. By 1968, TCS had purchased two IBM 1401s and one ICL 1903 and installed them at the Tata Computer Centre at Nirmal Building in Nariman Point, Mumbai. S. Ramadorai, who joined TCS as a young engineer in 1972, and went on to lead the company as Managing Director & CEO many years later, recalls, 'The young, talented TCS team behaved like a boisterous bunch from the Wild West . . . Agarwala realized that he needed a strong hand at the top, a sort of headmaster figure.'

During that period, Agarwala passed away and Kohli was appointed as director-in-charge at TCS. The company could not attract adequate data processing work from within the Tata Group, so it looked outside, to the big public sector undertakings, for business. To approach big companies like Hindustan Aeronautics, the Department of Atomic Energy and the Delhi Development Authority, TCS started to offer management consulting as a route to secure data processing assignments. It was a struggle in those years. However, talent acquisition did not falter at the fledgling TCS.

Even through the struggles, Kohli recruited top-flight youngsters—for example, S. Ramadorai, who held a master's from Stanford, the same Ramadorai who later succeeded Kohli as the CEO of TCS in 1996. One of the earliest assignments for Ramadorai was a posting in California to get American companies as clients for TCS. With a stern-looking boss like Kohli, Ramadorai had to learn soft skills to adapt. An important one was to disagree with his boss when necessary, without getting intimidated or being intimidated. On his part, Kohli seemed to be a master at challenging people to bring out the best in them. Kohli effused a 'can do' mindset, which was infectious among his talented young people.

TCS's contact with foreign companies led to an association with Burroughs Corporation, one of the big three computer manufacturers in the world at that time. To work with Burroughs, an energetic team of top-class Indian engineers had been built up, all exhibiting a gung-ho spirit.

Through the narrative so far, the reader would have noted that there was no past for TCS to reckon with, and there was a vagueness about the future shape of things; recruitment and talent density were influenced by the 'best from wherever', and team building was the key priority when it came to managing projects. As Ramadorai reminisced in his book (*The TCS Story*, Penguin, 2011), 'It helped that frugality and doing more with less were accepted in India, and the personal values of the team were aligned similarly . . . Frugal innovation may be a modern term, but the practice of it at TCS has been around a long time.'

By 1977, Tata had been associated with Burroughs for long enough to consider entering computer manufacture. TCS's parent company, Tata Sons, after weighing the risks, decided to implement the licence for the manufacture of computers in a new joint venture, Tata Burroughs. Here arose a strategic dilemma for the leaders of TCS.

Now there was TCS on the one hand, a 100 per cent Tata entity, and Tata Burroughs on the other, a part-Tata entity. Some were tempted to put them together, but Kohli made another strategic decision. They would be separate, collaborate when possible and compete when necessary. This was a significant decision, and as Ramadorai recalls in his book, 'Reflecting back, I believe that cutting the umbilical cord from Burroughs was the best thing that happened to us because it made TCS into a great entrepreneurial company.'

Remembering the period 1968–1996 as the years of 'building TCS', Ramadorai regards the subsequent period, 1996–2002, as the 'later years' and the period after 2002 for TCS as 'transforming for the future'. The TCS story demonstrates how long it takes to build a new entrepreneurial venture, how much persistence it takes, how key strategic decisions arise and how those decisions affect outcomes over the long term.

We think the story of TCS is instructive because its pioneering happened in more contemporary times, unlike the pioneering ventures of the Tatas in the early part of the previous century. TCS also illustrates the tremendous benefits of imparting to the company right from its infancy the durable values of frugality, solid talent management, winning customer strategies, team building and excruciating hard work to chase seemingly impossible goals.

These characteristics got embedded in the DNA of TCS over thirty-six years before the company became ready to go public through what was, at that time in 2004, India's largest public offering. There are silent and strategic lessons embedded in the story, so marvellously told by Ramadorai in his book. TCS made Tata a globally recognized brand name, though, of course, in the years that followed, several Tata companies entered the global markets through acquisitions. It would not be an exaggeration to say that just as Tata Steel and Tata Power marked the emergence of the 'industrial Tatas', the TCS IPO marked the emergence of the 'global Tatas'.

With hindsight, one can track the key inflection points in the progress and evolution of TCS. First came the development of the domestic business for computerization, an effort that TCS has carried out all through its existence. TCS owed a respectable percentage of its total business to the Indian market, as compared to most other software companies, which developed the more profitable overseas business. Second was separation of the 100 per cent TCS business from the Tata joint ventures with international tech companies—first with Burroughs, and later with IBM. Third was the nurturing of execution within the company. The bosses at competitor companies were known to make statements like, 'If Kohli called for people to rise or march, TCS-ers would willingly do so.' Fourth was the systematic and detailed preparation over three years for the company's IPO (initial public offering). Fifth was the continuous transformation effort at TCS to make it future-ready, an exercise largely led with great imagination by Ramadorai.

After Ramadorai's retirement, the rapid and disciplined growth of the company was led superbly and steadfastly for several years by N. Chandrasekaran (Chandra). During the period of Chandra's leadership, TCS scaled new heights of global excellence which has now made the company a formidable benchmark in its industry. Today, the company continues on its march of progress, having reinvented itself once again for the age of digital and artificial intelligence. The story of this immensely successful post-Ramadorai period deserves a separate narration.

3. The Rise and Rise of Consumer Brands

There was a time in the 1970s and 1980s when the Tata Group was regarded primarily as a manufacturing-led organization, with little focus on consumer marketing. Companies such as Tata Steel, Tata Motors, Tata Power and Tata Chemicals had established very high levels of excellence in production and business-to-business sales. However, consumer marketing was not their forte. They had prospered during an era where licensing was the norm and competition for the consumer's wallet was still in its infancy. In fact, by the early 1990s, the Tatas had sold off to Hindustan Unilever their stake in the only large consumer goods company they owned, Tata Oil Mills Company (TOMCO).

Today, in 2023, the canvas of the Tata Group has changed dramatically. Tata Steel, Tata Motors, Tata Power and Tata Chemicals continue to be prosperous companies. But in addition, the group dominates several consumer sectors, with brands that are amongst India's finest offerings. Here is a listing of some of its brands that are market leaders: Tata Salt, Tata Tea, Tetley Tea, Voltas air conditioners, Titan watches, Tanishq jewellery, Titan Eye Plus eyewear, Tata Motors cars and SUVs, Jaguar cars, Land Rover SUVs, Tata Tiscon steel, Tata Pravesh steel doors, Westside and Zudio stores for garments and lifestyle products, Croma stores for electronics, Tata Play DTH and broadband services and Taj Hotels.

This list of brands would be the envy of any global marketing giant. In fact, every second Indian uses some Tata brand today. That makes for a whopping total of over 700 million consumers in India who choose the Tata brand. What made this dramatic achievement possible? How did Tata consumer brands take over the Indian market over the past three decades?

First and foremost, most of the Tata brands focused significantly on building differentiated product or service offerings that appealed strongly to consumers by delivering sharply to their needs. Then these brands created layers of emotional appeal. They also built strong distribution networks to create consumer access. Most importantly, they offered consistently high product and service quality. In doing all this and more, they leveraged the strong trust that the Tata brand enjoys across the country.

A good illustration of this strategy is Tata Tea. It was a latecomer in the Indian packaged tea market, which was dominated by Hindustan Unilever's Brooke Bond and Lipton brands. Tata Tea changed the game by doing things differently from the time it launched in the mid-1980s. It used teas from its own plantations, packed these teas on its own estates to retain their freshness and used flexible packaging material that kept the freshness intact until the consumer opened the pack. By doing all this, it could position its teas on the platform of 'asli taazgi' or 'real freshness'—an attribute that consumers sought in their morning cup of tea—which no other brand had offered until then.

Tata Tea went on to develop distinctive blends of tea for every Indian region, based on consumer preferences, and adapted to different tea brewing methods. Once again, these customized offerings differentiated the brand from most of its other national competitors. As the years passed, many more differentiated variants of Tata Tea were developed through constant product innovation. For instance, one such hugely popular variant is Tata Tea Gold, which uses 15 per cent long-leaf tea in its blend to deliver aroma in addition to freshness.

To add emotive differentiation and appeal, Tata Tea built a strong advertising platform called 'Jaago Re' (Wake up), where it urged consumers to wake up to their civic responsibilities in addition to waking up with their favourite cup of tea. This is perhaps amongst the most iconic advertisements created in modern India. It has worked particularly well because consumers see this platform as a natural fit with the Tata brand, which has always been associated in their minds with nation-building. In recent times, Tata Tea has built further on its differentiation by customizing its packaging for each state in the country, thus cementing its strong emotive appeal.

In its early years, Tata Tea also shared a low-cost direct distribution system with Tata Salt, which enabled it to reach the far corners of the country very efficiently.

This also enabled the brand to offer competitive pricing and excellent value to consumers. Affordability for every market segment remains a hallmark of Tata Tea to this day. Later, the brand adopted this distribution system to meet the emerging needs of conventional and modern trade channels, and now E-commerce too.

Most importantly, ever since its launch the brand has emphasized the highest levels of quality. Blends of tea would be repeatedly tasted by expert tea tasters to ensure that they met the required taste, flavour and colour norms without fail. In fact, consistent quality has been the cornerstone of Tata Tea's consumer appeal. This has created a virtuous cycle, by reinforcing consumer perception that Tata can always be trusted for its commitment to quality.

It is on the back of such a robust strategy that Tata Tea has grown from a negligible presence in the mid-1980s to become a strong national player in the Indian packaged tea market, a well known and greatly admired name across India today. Today, it is very close to Hindustan Unilever in terms of market share. This is no mean feat, given that Unilever is one of the world's most powerful and successful consumer goods companies.

All the other successful consumer brands of the Tata Group have similar stories to tell, though the specific narrative may vary in each case. Let's consider branded garments, a very different market product from packaged tea. For Westside, the Tata brand which competes in this market, differentiation is centred on product styling and design, as well as on a beautiful shopping experience at its stores that are like theatres for fashion. Agile innovation ensures constant newness for consumers, which is an important need in the fashion and lifestyle category. Wide access has resulted from taking Westside across the country using an asset-light business model. An expert buying system and a well-oiled supply chain ensures efficiency at all points.

The consumer reposes their trust in Westside because, in addition to all the above-mentioned functional features which appeal, they know it is a Tata enterprise. Tata is a symbol of trust, a brand which will stand by them and never knowingly let them down. When the customer experiences the excellent quality, styling and overall value offered by Westside, this perception continues to grow even stronger in their mind.

These two examples—Tata Tea and Westside—provide a brief overview of the strategic path taken by most consumer brands of the Tata Group. The building blocks of such a strategy have typically included identification of key consumer needs, development of differentiated products or services to meet these needs, creation of wide and inclusive access and delivery of consistently high quality and value to consumers. Interestingly, while most of the major Tata brands have remained remarkably consistent in their appeal, specific elements of strategy have evolved over the years with each brand, based on learnings from previous hits and misses as well as the changing needs of consumers.

All these attributes sit on top of the firm foundation of the Tata brand and the trust that it has earned over the past several decades. In fact, this is the overarching strategic rationale for the Tata Group's entry and growth in diverse consumer markets in India—a strong brand that is synonymous with trust. Not merely that, this is a brand that can successfully extend into multiple consumer sectors because the trust it commands emanates from ideas that have universal appeal, such as integrity, nation building and excellence, rather than from just expertise in any specific industry.

6

Persistence

'*Nothing worthwhile is achieved without deep thought and hard work*'—J.R.D. Tata in a letter to K.C. Bhansali in 1965

This quotation from a letter that J.R.D. Tata wrote to a schoolteacher, K.C. Bhansali, strikes a chord with most of us. It captures a very middle-class virtue, whereby many forms of success are attributable to thoughtful planning and hard work. For most people, this statement is unexceptionable and indisputable when it comes to the middle-class aspiration to rise and prosper.

When it comes to pioneering entrepreneurship, is there an additional aspect or quality that is required? The goal being pursued may be good or bad, sustainable or unsustainable, materialistic for the self or noble for society. Once events pan out, if they are positive, history applauds the vision of the entrepreneur. If there is a lack of success, or worse still if there is a financial misadventure, history is prone to attribute it to the stupidity and folly of the entrepreneur. Is there a human quality or a skill of character that helps ensure positive outcomes, even though success can never be guaranteed? We think persistence is one such quality.

There are three narrations in this chapter accompanying this essay, all pertaining to the quality of persistence among the Tata Group leaders over the several decades.

The first relates to the dogged persistence of Jamsetji in the matter of what must have been a pipe dream in his days—the establishment of a national institution of sciences and higher learning for Indians. This grew into the Indian Institute of Science (IISc) in Bangalore, but it took about twenty years from conceptualization to inauguration. That period was marked by Jamsetji's insistence and advocacy that the colonial government support his intentions and plans. When he faced resistance within British India, he did not hesitate to take his case to the senior government officials in London, where he managed to find greater support. Since Jamsetji was on his deathbed before the idea could crystallize, he charged his son Dorabji with the task of completing the project after his time. This Dorabji did, with a filial sense of duty. The persuasive powers of Jamsetji must have been like those of IBM founder Thomas Watson Sr, of whom it was said, 'Watson's powers of persuasion were awesome. Not only could he persuade customers to buy his products, he could persuade his employees that they were capable of exceeding their own expectations. He could persuade men of great wealth and power to do things they did not want to do.'[1]

The second relates to the turnaround and technology advancement of India's first soda ash manufacturing factory at Tata Chemicals in Mithapur. The remarkable and persistent character of Darbari Seth, a brilliant chemical engineer, underpins the denouement of this story. It is appropriate to recall that during the 1950s, soda ash manufacture was a proprietary technology, dominated by global chemical majors like Solvay and ICI. The story displays the highs and lows of the plant at Mithapur, but what shines through is the resolve of the company that what will be good for the local community and for the nation must be pursued single-mindedly.

The third narrative pertains to our contemporary times, when a tenacious TAS officer, Xerxes Desai, persisted with his dream of introducing branding in the huge but largely unbranded market of jewellery in India. This adventure met with resistance from even within the Tata Group (disclosure: one of the authors, Gopal, had expressed his reservations about it!). Xerxes Desai's persistence was, no doubt, rooted in his knowledge of the market opportunity, but also in the spin-off benefits to customers and to the large labour force employed in the jewellery ecosystem. One of the authors, Harish, was intimately associated with this story during his career, as a senior member of the management team of the jewellery business. There was surely a deeper inspiration in Xerxes Desai than just making profits by entering this business. In an unrelated but relevant context, Henry Ford is reported to have said, 'I will build a car for the great multitude, constructed of the best materials by the best men to be hired after the simplest designs that modern engineering can devise.'[2]

All three stories have a common thread: that the goal being pursued with persistence had reasonable profits as a motive, but the impact of success was much bigger and long-lasting, over generations. In other words, there was persistence backing a positive long-term vision. Contrast this with some well-known examples from political history, such as the motives of Adolf Hitler.

Hitler was, by all accounts, confirmed in his ideology that the post-First-World-War problems that Germany was beset with had three origins: first, the self-centred attitude of the Weimar officials after the defeat in the war; second, the deep wounding of the German national psyche after the humiliations of the previous periods; third, the lack of racial Aryan purity among the population of the country at that time. Through his energy, demagoguery and actions, he went about correcting what he perceived to be the fatal flaws that weighed down his country. He persisted as far as he could, but history does not judge him well at all, because his motives were evil. There were a few strands of similarity, though they were far from identical to this German situation, in the motives of America in entering and prolonging the Vietnam war, or of the Soviet Union in embarking on its long Afghanistan war.

It would appear that the neeyat (strategic intent) in any action has a vital connection with whether persistence is later judged to be a virtue or a vice. Apply this principle to the so-called robber barons, many of whom were contemporaries of Jamsetji, and you will see that history now judges many of them quite differently from how Jamsetji is regarded today.

It is conjectured that the term originated in the Middle Ages, referring to the noblemen who functioned as feudal warlords and were literally 'robber barons'. By the nineteenth century, the term came to be applied to businessmen who were engaged in unethical and monopolistic practices, used corrupt political influences, faced almost no business regulation and amassed enormous wealth. Some of the more famous names that come to mind are Cornelius Vanderbilt, Andrew Carnegie, J.P. Morgan and John D. Rockefeller, all of whom were persistent leaders. Although this unfavourable soubriquet got attached to their names, they were also portrayed as self-made men who had helped to build the nation and create jobs for people.

The study of business management as a professional qualification has its own history. Harvard Business School, amongst a few others, had acquired a high reputation for such training and education. Around the 1920s, Dean Wallace Donham implored American businessmen to follow a form of stakeholder capitalism. He pleaded for a socially responsible stakeholder approach rather than a shareholder-focused approach. Dean Donham's pitch must be viewed in the context of his institution drawing elite, pre-selected entrants in their twenties—a group which could be assumed was more intent on making money than inclined to philosophical thought.

It is appropriate to emphasize that while the radical activists and media of this period portrayed all businessmen as ruthless, profit-seeking monsters, the reality was different. Many businesses were run by families or small business entrepreneurs who, more often than not, participated in their community through their individual community-reach activities. Even the so-called robber barons established a solid reputation as socially contributing members of their society. In general, they were law-abiding people with a sense of fairness and honesty, though none was flawless.

Coming to Indian entrepreneurs, this is not the place to comment on their social awareness and contributions. Suffice it to note that there is a long tradition of mercantile social contribution through the establishment of schools, welfare institutions, and towards medical aid and the general well-being of employees and the community. The key point to note may well be that persistence can be judged to be a virtue when there are also these three criteria in place:

- The founder or early founder acts and behaves with a sense of community, apart from seeking profits.
- The inevitable flaws of the early founders are few in number, far outstripped by their virtuous behaviours and actions.
- They have implemented a method to pass on their philosophy and bunch of practices to the succeeding generations.

Harvard Professor Rosabeth Moss Kanter proposed a twelve-point guideline to decide when to persist and when to quit.[3] The guidelines are in the form of questions that illustrate to the practitioner the way ahead:

1. Are the initial reasons for the effort still valid?
2. Would the situation get worse if this effort was stopped?
3. Are leaders still enthusiastic, committed, and focused on the effort?
4. Have critical deadlines been met?

These are valid guidelines, but they are heavily focused on the transactional aspects of the decision in question. The authors of this book advocate, in addition, a broader envelope that concerns the neeyat, the strategic intent.

As every golfer knows, once you stand on the tee box the transaction matters (swing, stance, posture), but what also matters is the intent behind how the next hole after the tee shot will be played. Read on, for three inspiring stories of persistence, all with the right intent.

Stories of Persistence

1. Creation of the IISc, Bangalore

In the year 1889, Jamsetji Tata heard a speech delivered by Lord Reay, the governor of Bombay, which inspired him to think about creating India's first university for higher education and research in science. This institution, which we know today as IISc, eventually opened more than twenty years later, in 1911. Sandwiched into those long years lies a story of incredible determination and persistence.

Lord Reay had pointed out in his speech that true higher education in India required universities that focused on teaching and research. This was essential to inspire deep learning and to impart strength and self-reliance to future generations of Indians. At that time, the few universities which India had were purely examining bodies. As Jamsetji pondered over what he had heard, he wondered why India should not have a world-class university. He also came to the conclusion that higher education, particularly in science and technical subjects, was essential for the development of his beloved country—

141

just as the great universities of the Western world had
been in Europe and the USA, triggering technological
progress and development there.

Jamsetji realized, however, that the creation of such a
university was an ambitious project, requiring not just vast
resources but also government support and approval. In
addition, he was an industrialist and education was not
his field of expertise. But by the early 1890s, he appears to
have decided that he would make this happen, no matter
what hurdles he had to cross.

The first such challenge was to achieve a full grasp of
the subject. To get this done, he identified and appointed
a brilliant young man, Burjorji Padshah, who had
himself worked at Cambridge University. Jamsetji waited
patiently as Padshah undertook a detailed first-hand
study of the great universities of Europe and America.
Padshah submitted his findings eighteen months later,
including a recommendation that the John Hopkins
University of Baltimore, USA, was a good benchmark for
India to follow.

As soon as Jamsetji obtained the results of this survey,
he wrote to Lord Reay in November 1896, spelling out
his proposal for the establishment of a university for the
sciences. Jamsetji then developed the proposal further, and
in September 1898 he made a public announcement that
took India by storm.

He announced that he was offering his own properties
worth Rs 30 lakh for the establishment of a university
of higher education for Indians. These properties would
yield an annual income of Rs 1,25,000, which would go
towards the funding of the institution. This was a fabulous

sum of money in those days, and it constituted a significant portion of Jamsetji's overall wealth.

This extraordinary announcement drew widespread praise. Writing in *The Hindu* newspaper, a prominent citizen said, 'Mother Bharati has long been crying for a man among her children, and in Mr. Tata, she has found the son of her heart.'

It was clear, however, that the amount committed by Jamsetji, large as it was, would only be around half the sum required for establishing a world-class university. Jamsetji therefore applied himself to the challenge of raising the rest of the funds. Apart from reaching out directly to the wealthy princely states of the country, he also chose to pursue an unconventional route—by writing to Swami Vivekananda, a highly respected spiritual figure.

Jamsetji had earlier met Swami Vivekananda on a ship voyage from Japan to America a few years ago. Now, in November 1898, he wrote to him seeking his help in rousing people on the subject of this institute, by issuing an appeal to them. Within a few months, an article appeared in the *Prabuddha Bharata*, the monthly magazine started by Swamiji. This article strongly endorsed Jamsetji Tata's scheme and urged the entire nation to join in making it a success. Never before had a merchant and a monk come together in pursuit of such an enterprise.

The next hurdle was to get the project approved by the British government of India. To address this, Jamsetji formed a provisional committee comprising many well-regarded and knowledgeable people, who would help prepare an initial project report and representation that could be submitted to the Viceroy of India. This committee included the vice-chancellor of Bombay University, a judge of the Bombay High Court, the president of the Bombay Municipal Corporation and the editor of the *Times of India* newspaper. Clearly, Jamsetji was drawing upon some of the finest minds in his city to evolve the best possible proposal for the university.

However, the going was not easy. When the provisional committee met the viceroy, Lord Curzon, in 1899 to brief him about their project, they received a frosty response bordering on the negative. Curzon acknowledged Jamsetji Tata's generosity but wondered whether there would be enough students to justify the appointment of highly paid professors. He also expressed doubts as to whether the graduating students would be able to find appropriate jobs in the country. In addition, he did not think it would be right for the government to encourage princely states to contribute to such a project.

Jamsetji Tata sat quietly through this important meeting. If he was deeply disappointed, he did not show it. On the other hand, after the meeting, he told the members of the committee that there was no reason to be discouraged, even though some of them felt the Viceroy had thrown cold water on the scheme. He added that since Curzon was new to the country, perhaps he did not like to commit himself so early.

Most importantly, despite this apparent setback, Jamsetji kept his faith in the project because he believed fervently in the cause. He arranged for distribution of the committee's project report to educational experts throughout India, for their suggestions and critical comments. Broadly, the response of these experts was positive, albeit with some critical observations. He also kept alive the negotiations with the government, navigating some difficult conversations and offering to make any minor changes as required by the authorities. Simultaneously, he continued to work on seeking funds for the project.

On this last aspect, he met with success when the dewan of the princely state of Mysore, Sir Seshadri Iyer, whom Jamsetji knew from past interactions, suggested that Bangalore could be considered as the location for the university. He also conveyed a princely offer from the Maharaja of Mysore, who was keen to bring development to his kingdom through higher education. The Maharaja would provide 375 acres of land in Bangalore, a one-time grant of Rs 5 lakh towards construction of the institute as well as an annual subsidy towards its running. Soon thereafter, a similar competing offer also came from Mumbai, from Chabildas Lalloobhoy, one of the largest landowners in the city.

In the meanwhile, the British government of India suggested that the entire project be examined once again by a well-known scientist. Jamsetji agreed readily, and the provisional committee he had formed finalized the name of Professor William Ramsay, the famous chemist who later also won the Nobel Prize. Jamsetji agreed to bear all the expenses of Ramsay's visit and also to pay him a generous fee for the exercise. Ramsay visited India, spending over two months in the country and submitting his report. He too recommended Bangalore as the location for the institute and also provided his views on the initial departments and the staffing that could be considered. Ramsay also rejected the term 'university' for the institute because it did not cover all branches of knowledge. Jamsetji Tata, whose dream had been to create a university, saw the logic of Ramsay's recommendation, and the name finally accepted for the establishment was 'Indian Institute of Science'.

The battle had still not been won because the government of India, led by Lord Curzon, had rejected many of Ramsay's recommendations. Curzon thought that Ramsay's plan was too lavish, and in 1901 he appointed his own committee to re-examine the entire matter. This committee recommended a smaller institute of study and suggested Roorkee as the location. Curzon was also unwilling to provide the required financial support from the government, as recommended by Ramsay. It appeared that the government was dragging its feet on the project, and the new proposal of a smaller institute was, in any case, not in line with Jamsetji's vision of creating a world-class university for India.

Jamsetji Tata was made of sterner stuff. He now took his arguments to London. The year was 1902, and the authorities in London were preoccupied for several weeks with the coronation of King Edward VII. Jamsetji waited patiently until these festivities had concluded. He then met Lord George Hamilton, Secretary of State for India, and pressed the case for the institute once again. We do not know what exactly transpired at this meeting, but it is clear that soon afterwards, pressure from the India Office in London galvanized the government of India into action.

The government of India announced in May 1903 that they were prepared to make a contribution of £2,000 per year towards the institute, adding to the contributions of Jamsetji and the Maharaja of Mysore. In addition, the government also suggested a flexible method for completion of the required formalities for starting the institute. Suddenly there was light at the end of the tunnel, and it appeared that Jamsetji's dream would, after all these years, finally come true.

Unfortunately, Jamsetji Tata passed away the next year. However, a few months before his death, he wrote a codicil to his will re-emphasizing his financial commitment to the institute and binding his estate to carry out this undertaking once the institute received full sanction from the government.

It was then left to his elder son, Dorabji Tata, to take forward the final leg of discussions with Lord Curzon and the government of India. Later that year, the government accepted Sir William Ramsay's recommendations on the size, scale and location of the institute. It also agreed to make the required financial contribution as well. Within two years, staff were appointed, and in 1909 the vesting orders were issued. In 1911, the first students were admitted to the institute, in the departments of chemistry and electro-technology.

Today the IISc enjoys a formidable reputation across the world and is India's top-rated university of higher studies and research in science. Through its portals and classrooms have passed some of India's most eminent scientists. This magnificent educational institution stands as a tribute not merely to Jamsetji Tata's abiding love for India, but also to his dogged determination and persistence in pursuing such an ambitious project which faced so many challenges over so many years.

2. Tata Chemicals and Darbari Seth

In the year 1937, the Maharaja of Baroda, Sayajirao Gaekwad, approached the Tata Group with a suggestion that Tatas could consider helping with an industrial project designed to make salt and inorganic chemicals in his kingdom. This project, called Okha Salt Works, located by the seaside in the town of Mithapur in Gujarat, had been founded several years ago by a chemical engineer and entrepreneur named Kapilram Vakil. However, it had now run into serious difficulties and was on the verge of shutting down.

The Tata Group assessed this project and concluded that there was indeed a potential business opportunity here, if things were done right. Equally importantly, the Tatas were seized of the national importance of this project, because ordinary salt and essential chemicals, such as soda ash, were the monopoly of foreign companies at that time. If India needed to be self-reliant in these important products, an indigenous effort such as this one had to succeed.

Thus, a company called Tata Chemicals was launched in 1939, after the acquisition of Okha Salt Works. J.R.D. Tata had just become chairman of the Tata Group in 1938, and he backed this important venture fully. However, this was not the best of times, because the Second World War soon broke out. Amongst other things, the onset of the war resulted in the dislocation of the machinery ordered for Tata Chemicals, leading to confusion and delays.

In addition, the entrepreneur Kapilram Vakil (who had stayed on with the company after it had been acquired) and his team struggled to develop the technology for manufacturing soda ash on the required scale. This code was a closely guarded secret known only to a few companies globally. Unless Tata Chemicals was able to master this technology, the company would find it very difficult to survive.

Initially, the company sought help from Chinese experts. Then an American expert, Zola Deutsche, was brought in to help. He reached the conclusion that although the basic raw materials for soda ash manufacture were available in and around Mithapur, the lack of fresh water and coal, as well as the sub-optimally small plant capacity, made the project unviable. In fact, he advised J.R.D. Tata to say, 'You are in the wrong place and in the wrong business; the sooner you get out the better.' J.R.D. Tata is reported to have retorted, 'This is not the first time we have done this. When we go to a place we arouse hopes in people, and we expect to fulfil those hopes.'

In other words, the Tatas were committed, and the company *had* to succeed. The leadership team was, however, somewhat fatigued by its lack of success up to that point and was on the verge of approaching yet another foreign company for help when JRD came across a brilliant young chemical engineer in a business review meeting held in 1951. His name was Darbari Seth, and he had joined Tata Chemicals in 1947. He was passionate, and as he presented his ideas, he argued forcefully that Indians could do as well if not better than foreigners in evolving and implementing the required design for a soda ash manufacturing plant.

His fearlessness, optimism and his ideas instinctively struck a chord with JRD, who had a keen eye for identifying talent. JRD advised the company leadership to put Seth effectively in charge of the soda ash plant. Until then, Seth's ideas had largely been ignored by the management. Many years later JRD would say, 'I perceived he just may be the person to get the (manufacturing plant) moving.'

Darbari Seth moved quickly, by sending his designs for the soda ash plant to J.R.D. Tata. JRD advised him to have these designs vetted by Zola Deutsche, the American expert. Seth was 'deeply hurt' that his chairman did not have full faith in him. Nonetheless, he travelled to New York and met Zola Deutsche there, because he saw this as an essential step to success.

There he appears to have convinced the American expert that his designs were absolutely the right way to proceed. Only a week later, Zola Deutsche happened to meet JRD, who was visiting New York, and told him. 'You must give this young man more self-confidence, Mr. Tata, because someone who can design like that does not need to consult me or anyone else.'

With this endorsement on his side, Darbari Seth obtained the required approvals for his technical designs. His team then went ahead with the execution of the designs. In 1957, he launched a hugely ambitious project for large-scale expansion of the soda ash plant to 400 tonnes per day, after having made a presentation to J.R.D. Tata and the management board of the company on why this was the right step ahead. This step would require a huge leap of faith to take, but JRD supported Seth.

The project was duly christened four hundred tonnes programme (FHTP)—a name that unambiguously spelt out the target. A project of this scale in India was mind boggling at that time, but the objective was clear—a successful plant of this size would ensure the future prosperity of Tata Chemicals.

To take forward this project, Darbari Seth first built a core team that was technically competent, passionate, committed and resilient. They put all distractions aside. Mohan Vadagama, who worked in the engineering drawing office at that time, has recalled how they would be at work at between 6 a.m. and 7 a.m., often sharing breakfast and skipping lunch because there was so little time. This was a complex project, with many moving parts, and requiring integration across thirteen different plants.

Darbari Seth and his team worked on resolving every element of this complexity with great determination. Simultaneously, they focused on using cost-efficient indigenous materials for construction, particularly because imported materials would have cost twice as much. A strong sense of purpose—to make Mithapur achieve its true potential—fuelled their resolve. Their persistence paid off handsomely when, after many intermediate milestones, the 400-tonne target was eventually reached in 1964. Here was an achievement without precedent, and Mithapur rejoiced.

Even as Darbari Seth and his team were working their way to success, yet another huge challenge appeared on the horizon. One of the big issues Mithapur had faced ever since the inception of the factory was the lack of adequate fresh water for its manufacturing operations and for the people living in the township. In 1962, this situation reached crisis proportions when Mithapur faced a drought. The rains failed and it was predicted that both the freshwater lakes that supplied the town would run out of water by October that year. The crisis was so severe that there was even talk of evacuation of the town.

Darbari Seth led from the front to resolve this challenge. To begin with, he set out his position in the matter, which was quite simple and wonderfully defiant. 'Mithapur will shut down over my dead body,' he said.

He put together a team and a war room that had a single-point agenda—to ensure that Mithapur continued to operate without any disruption throughout this terrible period of drought. This team came up with more than 200 ideas spanning three broad themes—conservation of freshwater, substitution of freshwater with seawater wherever this was feasible and production of freshwater within the manufacturing complex. These ideas were then implemented on a war footing.

One such idea was the laying of nearly six miles of pipes to carry freshwater from wells to the Mithapur water works. Another idea was the declaration of a 'lakeless week' for the factory and town, when no water at all was drawn from the lakes. The success of this symbolic but powerful move proved that what was perceived to be impossible could actually be done. The overall consumption of water was reduced, through multiple measures, from 22 lakh gallons per day to 5 lakh gallons.

Through relentless execution of all these ideas, Darbari Seth and his team ensured that production at their plant was unaffected, and the township also obtained its essential requirement of water. In fact, Mithapur did not receive rains for two more years but the plant continued to function throughout this period. The team had pulled off a miracle. The success of these ideas had not just protected the company in the short-term but had also insulated Tata Chemicals from the ravages of drought forever thereafter. Once again, Mithapur rejoiced.

In the subsequent years, Tata Chemicals successfully navigated many more difficulties and achieved several proud milestones under Darbari Seth's inspiring leadership. He became the company's first managing director in 1970, and continued to steward the fortunes of this very successful Tata company until his retirement about twenty-five years later.

Darbari Seth was undoubtedly a brilliant technocrat, but what marked him out equally were his fearlessness and persistence in frontally addressing all the challenges that his team and he encountered with a constant sense of urgency and a 'nothing is impossible' attitude. In doing this, he repeatedly made the impossible possible.

3. Belief and Resilience: The Early Years of Tanishq

Today, Tanishq is by far the strongest jewellery brand in India. This brand evokes trust amongst millions of Indian women. It has also transformed the huge jewellery market in India. However, did you know that this business was on the verge of being shut down in its early years? It is only belief and persistence on the part of the leadership that saved it from oblivion.

Let's turn the clock back a few decades. Titan Watches, a company founded in 1984 as a joint venture between the Tata Group and the Tamil Nadu government, had achieved remarkable success in the wristwatches market in India. With a stunning range of quartz watches and superlative marketing, Titan had quickly captured more than a 50 per cent share of the market and had become a household name in the country. Leading the charge at Titan was a Tata veteran, Xerxes Desai, who had founded the company with the strong support of J.R.D. Tata. Riding high on the success of Titan watches, the company won many honours, and Xerxes was soon perceived as an inspired marketing genius.

But soon there came along a small twist in this tale. Titan watches used many imported components, which required it to spend in foreign exchange. In 1991, when India ran into a serious foreign exchange crisis, the cash-strapped government insisted that Titan earn its own foreign exchange through exports to fund its imports. What indigenous product could Titan possibly export?

After considerable discussion, Xerxes and his leadership team decided that jewellery could be a good category to pursue. The logic was simple. The world over, at the premium end, jewellers were also watch makers. Both watches and jewellery were products of exquisite design and personal adornment and required some common skill sets to make. In addition, it appeared that there was a large market for gold jewellery in Europe and the USA waiting to be tapped. Titan could export jewellery to these markets and earn the required foreign exchange.

To implement this project, Titan invested a large sum of money (around Rs 65 crore) in a large, state-of-the-art jewellery manufacturing plant at Hosur, an industrial township in Tamil Nadu but closer to Bangalore city. Soon, exquisite jewellery designed for European women, and made with 18-carat fine gold (which was the gold standard in European countries) began rolling out from this plant.

Unfortunately, things did not pan out as planned. Due to a global economic downturn, the demand for fine gold jewellery came down significantly in Europe and the USA. Women in those countries began shopping for more inexpensive steel-and-gold looks. Titan's fine jewellery was just not competitive enough in this new reality. In addition, within three years the government of India stopped insisting that Titan earn its own foreign exchange through exports because the Indian economy had recovered remarkably after the 1991 reforms, and other industries such as IT services were now earning a lot of foreign exchange.

Recalling those days, Xerxes Desai has said:

So, here we had a big jewellery factory and no overseas market worth the effort of developing. This was an expensive plant, with expensive people. The European market for gold jewellery had shrunk, demand from those quarters had declined and it no longer made sense to compete in that space. That is when we turned to the Indian market, and we thought of Tanishq.

In launching a jewellery brand in India, Xerxes Desai was greatly encouraged by the words of his mentor J.R.D. Tata, whom he had consulted during the early days of the jewellery project. In fact, JRD had been quite positive in his response to the project. However, the other directors of the Tata Group were not so convinced. In fact, there was deep scepticism among many Tata directors, that jewellery, a business that flourished in the unorganized sector, could

ever be successful in the hands of a corporate body like
Titan. There were also pockets of cynicism within the very
successful watches business in Titan. Would it not make far
more strategic sense to strengthen the profitable watches
portfolio rather than expend a lot of resources in launching
a jewellery brand in India, in a category where no national
brand had ever succeeded before?

Xerxes Desai reflected on all these comments
and discussed them with his senior team. However,
one indisputable fact stood out for him—the market
opportunity in India was too large to ignore. At that time
the size of the market exceeded Rs. 50,000 crore annually
(today is nearly eight times that size). In addition, Titan's
proven design, marketing and manufacturing skills, as
well as its Tata parentage, could be invaluable assets in
addressing the jewellery market. Leaders are often defined
by the courageous decisions that they make. Xerxes Desai,
driven by his belief in the Indian consumer, decided to
launch Tanishq as a jewellery brand in India.

In 1996, the first Tanishq store opened at Cathedral
Road in Chennai. Soon stores were opened in the other
big metros of India—Delhi, Mumbai and Bangalore. These
were impressive and opulent stores, inspired by the luxury-
brand stores of Europe. Within these stores were displayed
beautiful, fine 18-carat jewellery studded with precious
gems. The product range was primarily gem-set (studded)
jewellery of the kind that Titan had begun exporting to
Europe a few years ago. Studded jewellery also held the
potential of far greater profit margins. Plain gold jewellery
was a very small part of the offering. The strategy, in Xerxes
Desai's own words, was to make Tanishq 'a composite

Indian avatar of Cartier, Tiffany, Asprey and even Ernest Jones, all rolled into one'.

However, elegant strategy developed in the rarefied air of CEOs' cabins soon faces the harsh reality of markets. The Tanishq stores and jewellery were beautiful, but the company soon noticed that one important person was missing. The customer.

Clara Lobo, who worked in the Tanishq store in Bandra, Mumbai, during those early days, recalls what it was like in 1997: 'We would wait for hours for a single customer to walk in. Often, a whole week would pass by in silence, and we would feel very depressed. Our performance was so poor that sometimes we even heard that this brand would be shut down.'

Clearly, the Indian woman had been totally unmoved by Tanishq. The reason soon became clear. Gold jewellery for Indian women was not merely a piece of adornment. It was her personal wealth, traditionally called *stridhan*. She was not willing to dilute this very important aspect of her life by buying 18-carat gold jewellery, which was, in her perception, far less valuable than 22-carat gold. In fact, 22-carat gold had been for centuries the accepted standard for jewellery in in India. Why would the Indian woman change this? In her view, 18-carat gold jewellery, gem-set or otherwise, was unsuitable for traditional Indian occasions, such as weddings and festivals. In addition, the Tanishq showrooms with their opulence and western-style jewellery just did not connect with her. In fact, they intimidated her. 'Not for me', was her reaction.

Xerxes Desai's initial strategy had failed miserably. The marketers of Titan, who had been celebrated for conquering the watches market in India, had been brought down to earth. More importantly, the lack of customers meant that little was being sold. This, combined with the high fixed costs of the opulent stores and a huge jewellery factory, led to severe recurring losses.

Pressure mounted on Xerxes to exit the business, from some directors in the Tata Group as well as within the company. Ishaat Hussain, who represented the Tata Group on Titan's board of directors, wrote to Xerxes expressing his strong concern about the mounting losses. Ishaat recalls his personal reservations about whether a business such as jewellery could ever lend itself to 'scale, corporate management and factory manufacture'. The recurring losses now further re-emphasized this view.

Within Titan too people were worried. Some observers were of the opinion that there was no light at the end of the tunnel for the company and Tanishq would only bleed away the hard-earned profits of the watches business. In addition, around that time, the company had gone through yet another misadventure in Europe, this time in watches, compounding the financial stress.

However, to the credit of the Tata Group, they left the final decision on the jewellery business to Xerxes Desai and the board of directors of Titan Industries. There were opposing voices on the board—Ishaat Hussain had his reservations about the project while another Tata director, Jamshed Bhabha, voiced his support to it. Some directors wanted Xerxes to cut his losses and sell the business, whereas others, including representatives of the Tamil Nadu government, were supportive.

The decision thus came down to Xerxes himself. He was in a tough spot. He consulted his senior management team, which included Vasant Nangia, Jacob Kurian and Bhaskar Bhat. After calm and thoughtful discussions extending over many sessions, he reached the conclusion that the business had huge potential, but that errors in strategy and execution had led to the current situation. The need of the hour was to craft the right strategy—a sound consumer proposition that appealed to Indian women, and very good execution.

Many years later, Xerxes Desai would recall this difficult time:

> Yes, there certainly was pressure to hive off this business. There was mixed support from some people in the Tatas. There was also an opinion that the jewellery business could only be run by family jewellers, that it could never be corporatized.
>
> But I was firm in my view, and I said that any such hiving off or closure would happen over my dead body. We saw the huge opportunity, we had belief and we persisted.

Having decided to move forward, Tanishq now made two big changes to its consumer offerings. In 1999, it introduced a wide range of 22-carat gold jewellery. It also ensured that many of the products were inspired by Indian looks. In making both these changes, Tanishq aligned its offerings with the key needs of a large segment of Indian women. The brand retained some offerings in 18-karat studded jewellery, but this was no longer the primary focus.

In addition, through market surveys, the team spotted a unique opportunity for disrupting the jewellery category. They found that a large number of unscrupulous jewellers were cheating their customers by offering less caratage of gold than promised. For instance, a jeweller would promise 22-carat gold, but the jewellery he sold would actually be of 17-karat gold, which was far less expensive, and the layperson would not know the difference. If Tanishq could bring home this point to customers, it could build its own differentiated position as a brand that offered exactly what it promised, a brand that customers could trust.

To do this, Tanishq pioneered one of the greatest innovations in the Indian jewellery market—the 'Karatmeter'. This instrument used the science of spectroscopy to measure the purity or caratage of gold in three minutes. A senior member of Xerxes Desai's team, M.S. Shantaram, had come across this machine during a visit to Europe. Xerxes and team were quick to spot its potential. It was branded 'Karatmeter' and placed in the Tanishq showrooms. Tanishq now invites customers to visit their stores and check the purity of their own gold jewellery on these Karatmeters, at no cost.

Tens of thousands of customers soon tested their jewellery on these Karatmeters and found, to their dismay, that the caratage of their products was actually far less than what their family jewellers had promised. They wept, and they felt cheated. Many of them decided to shift their loyalties to Tanishq. Tanishq became the brand that Indian women could trust, and the brand's Tata parentage further reinforced this proposition.

This was the beginning of Tanishq's success. However, while these significant changes—the right product portfolio and the proposition of trust—were essential ingredients, they were not the entire recipe for success. The business had to become far larger if it had to sustain and generate the required economic returns. To do this, it had to appeal to millions of young Indian women and break the perception that it was an expensive, niche brand. It had to evolve the appropriate jewellery designs for every region of India. It had to build a tight supply chain and find a way to grow, in a manner that was not capital intensive. It had to execute to precision. And, most importantly, it had to build strong belief in the team that the business was here to stay, and would succeed big time.

Many of these ingredients began coming together seamlessly after Xerxes Desai appointed one of his best senior managers, Jacob Kurian, to head the Tanishq business. Jacob drove a strong belief in Tanishq amongst all the stakeholders, even as he worked tirelessly to put all these building blocks in place. Soon thereafter, in 2002, Xerxes Desai retired and Bhaskar Bhat became the managing director of Titan. Jacob continued to work closely with Bhaskar, built a super-committed team and convinced them that they could achieve extraordinary things at Tanishq. Once again, sharp strategy, combined with great persistence and superb execution, was key to the success that was achieved.

Under Jacob's charge, Tanishq became a profitable business and a successful brand. The light now began shining bright at the end of the tunnel. Ishaat Hussain, the Tata director who had written to Xerxes Desai several years ago expressing his reservations about the jewellery business, recalls that this was the stage at which he changed his initial views about Tanishq and became far more confident about its future. One of the authors of this book, Harish, was privileged to be a member of Jacob's core team at Tanishq, and had also succeeded him as the COO of the business.

In the later years, leaders such as C.K. Venkatraman and Ajoy Chawla took Tanishq to new heights. They have addressed multiple challenges and opportunities along the way, with the same spirit of persistence that Xerxes Desai had demonstrated way back in the early days of Tanishq. But that is the subject of another interesting story.

7

Principles

'We do not claim to be more unselfish, more generous, or more philanthropic than other people. But we think we started on sound and straightforward business principles, considering the interests of the shareholders as our own, and the health and welfare of our employees, the sure foundation of our success'—Jamsetji Tata, in a speech delivered in 1895

Conducting the affairs of an enterprise with a set of constant principles to guide it over a couple of centuries is a very tall order. After all, principles may change over time, with social mores. Different generations of leaders may have contradicting perceptions of the principles that should guide them. The ecosystem in which the corporation functions surely changes rapidly over a couple of centuries. Above all, human nature being what it is, aberrations are ever so likely, whereby the actions of leaders over the generations can be viewed through multiple lenses.

These elements broadly set out the difficulty for a company in 'being good' all the time, consistently and reliably. It is well-nigh impossible.

There are three stories that accompany this essay. The first is about the dilemma the house of Tata faced when the market environment for steel altered dramatically after the First World War. Cash flows in the business deteriorated rapidly, to the point where the company's ability to pay the workers their salaries was threatened. This story tells of how Dorabji Tata and his wife Meherbai placed their entire personal wealth, including the famous Jubilee Diamond, as collateral to raise money from banks to disburse the workers' salaries. The story shows that statutory obligations apart, moral obligations too played a role in the decisions made by the family.

The second story dwells on some of the ethical dilemmas that J.R.D. Tata wrestled with. As can be observed, a dilemma can be resolved through multiple possible solutions. The solution chosen by a leader has to sit in harmony with his or her values and sense of ethics. In another person's perspective, there could well be an alternative solution that is better.

The third story is more contemporary and relates to the tenure of Ratan Tata. The Tata Finance episode was a shock for the house of Tata. Of course, such a shock could affect any enterprise. What that enterprise does after receiving the shock shows what moral compass it is made of. In this story, you will read about how principles guided the response of the Tata Group, and how the group in fact emerged stronger from this unfortunate episode.

In this part of the book, when we use the expression 'principles', we imply those set of values that do not change over time. The essence of principled behaviour is a bit like the Gangotri described earlier in the book. The firm adopts those principles that are characterized by simplicity, purity and immutability, just like the core philosophy of a religion or of spirituality. As this Gangotri flows over time and different terrains, interpretations start to develop, followed by rituals and symbolism.

The modern narrative sometimes suggests that high visibility and market capitalization automatically imply a principled approach within the enterprise. We all know that this need not be true. Conversely, when confronted with a single aberration, the corporation should not be dissed as being 'like any other, devoid of principles and morality'.

To run an enterprise with principles and by a moral compass, the leaders should, by and large, be following the immutable and consistent values that the enterprise stands for. The three Tata stories here seek to highlight this simple perspective. Further, the enterprise does not have to be a large, fast-growing or high-profile entity to adopt such principles. All forms of enterprise can, and should, strive to do so.

Since the industrial revolution, size, growth, and, more recently, market capitalization, have all become monikers for corporate greatness. Is this method of assessing corporate greatness really valid? Are there no 'great' companies that are not giant by size but are giant by reputation and by their contribution to society?

A book by journalist Bo Burlingham is worth a read. It is a chronicle of 'small giants' that, quietly under the radar, have rejected the pressure of endless growth to focus on more satisfying business goals. Consider as examples Conzerv India (sold to the French electrical major Schneider), Galaxy Surfactants (now a listed company) and Microland (a private global technology infrastructure services company, approaching its thirty-fifth anniversary, and four times recognized by Gartner Magic Quadrant). None of them is famous or perfect, but their business conduct appears exemplary! Maybe they qualify as Indian 'small giants'.

Indian economic development depends crucially on small enterprises and family-managed businesses. We focus on their distinguishing feature: family-managed businesses see reputation as their principal asset and currency. Every family may not do so, but many do. That is to be cheered. Families manage businesses for the legacy they are creating. Valuation is an outcome.

An example of a well-respected business group that follows these principles is Beit Binzagr in Saudi Arabia, which one of the authors of this book, Gopal, has intimate knowledge of. The story of Beit Binzagr has already been narrated in an earlier chapter of this book. Their principles have been a strong foundation of their sustained success and longevity. Beit Binzagr is thus a good example of sound neeyat.

The examples of these 'small giants' are evidence that neeyat is relevant for all enterprises—family-run, promoter-driven or multinational. India is right to celebrate big firms, but it must also cheer its valuable small giants.

The accompanying three stories, which are set over the time period of a century, and showcase the difficult choices made by leaders from three different generations, illustrate the deep value of principles.

Stories of Principles

1. Saving Tata Steel

Tata Steel was one of the first great industrial enterprises conceptualized by Jamsetji Tata, founder of the Tata Group. Jamsetji believed that steel was essential for the development of a nation. Therefore he was of the view that India should not depend entirely on imports of steel, but should have its own integrated steel plant.

In taking forward the planning for this huge enterprise in the 1890s, Jamsetji Tata had to battle the scepticism of the British rulers of India. He succeeded in attracting to India one of the finest engineers from the USA, Charles Page Perin, to help with the required technology. After Jamsetji's demise in 1904, his son Dorabji Tata, who succeeded him as chairman of the Tata Group, took charge of the project. Dorabji also successfully raised the required capital in the Indian market—an unprecedented feat in itself—thus making Tata Steel a fully swadeshi enterprise.

By 1912, Tata Steel had begun production at its plant in Sakchi in eastern India (the town was later renamed

Jamshedpur, in honour of Jamsetji Tata). The steel was of excellent quality, thus proving the sceptics wrong. During the First World War, the company supplied over 1,500 miles of steel rails to the Allied war effort in Mesopotamia. Over 8,000 tons of steel shells were made in the open-hearth furnaces at Jamshedpur. The plant began running to full capacity on a twenty-four-hour schedule and still could not keep up with the demand, despite producing 1,50,000 tons of steel annually.

At this point, the leadership of the company—including Dorabji Tata and his partner R.D. Tata—analysed the emerging demand situation and came to the conclusion that after the war, India itself could absorb many times this amount of steel. By then Tata Steel was already supplying rails to Indian Railways. In addition, Tata Steel was also earning nice profits on the small consignments that it exported. In December 1916, Dorabji Tata was full of confidence as he spoke to his shareholders about the company's bumper earnings, production at the plant being 30 per cent over the original capacity and its order book being totally full.

Buoyed by this success, the company began considering a plan of expansion to meet the high current and future demand. Charles Page Perin, who was in charge of this planning, initially recommended to the directors of the company a gradual increase in steel capacity, from 1,50,000 tons to 2,25,000 tons a year. He considered this to be a safe and prudent plan.

However, Dorabji Tata had a far more dynamic and ambitious plan in mind. He spoke passionately to the directors about his father Jamsetji Tata's vision of a self-reliant and strong nation, which was at the heart of his dream for Tata Steel. He recommended a vast expansion programme, which would eventually supply India's entire requirements of steel. To begin with, this would entail an expansion of the steel-making capacity at Jamshedpur by five times. Dorabji also said he would raise all the required capital from Indian investors.

This ambitious expansion plan, called the 'TISCO greater extensions programme', began in right earnest by 1917. However, it ran into a number of difficulties. Tata Steel was compelled to purchase materials at high wartime prices. There were labour strikes in England and a shortage of skilled labour in India. In addition, the Indian rupee depreciated during this time. As a result, the capital cost of the expansion programme, which had been budgeted at Rs 6.8 crore, rose more than three times to Rs 19.6 crore. Additional funds had to be raised from the shareholders because the company's profits could not support such huge sums of expenditure.

And then, suddenly, after the First World War ended, the company's profits declined precipitously. This happened because of several factors. Belgium began dumping its steel at very low prices in the Indian market, which had no tariff protection at that time. In addition, Japan, which was Tata Steel's largest customer of pig iron, was hit by a huge earthquake (the Great Kanto earthquake) in 1923. One of the worst natural disasters ever to strike Japan, the earthquake reduced the country's financial capability to purchase steel.

By the end of 1923, demand for Tata Steel's products had fallen significantly and the company's profits had declined to nearly break-even levels. On the other hand, significant funds had been expended in expanding the plant. This led to a severe cash crunch, and some of the company's directors even suggested that it go to the British government of India with a request to be taken over by it. R.D. Tata, Dorabji's partner, rose in angry indignation when he heard this suggestion. He pounded his fists on the table and declared that such a day would never come as long as he lived.

While we do not know what thoughts went through R.D. Tata's mind when he said this, it is quite likely that he recalled Jamsetji Tata's objective in establishing Tata Steel—a swadeshi Indian steel company, dedicated to the nation. Instead, what Dorabji and he had in mind was an alternative plan to negotiate with the government to consider imposing reasonable tariffs that would protect Tata Steel from unfair competition from tariff-free European steel.

However, such a plan would take time to materialize, particularly because it involved government policy. In the meanwhile, Tata Steel continued to reel under its immediate miseries, with very little cash in hand to keep operations alive. Dorabji and R.D. Tata struggled to raise funds in the adverse post-war environment. Then, one day, in 1924, a telegram arrived from Jamshedpur at Dorabji Tata's table, bearing bad news. It simply said that there was not enough money left to pay wages to the employees of Tata Steel.

Would the fledgling company survive, or would it be forced to shut down? Would Jamsetji Tata's dreams and visions of creating India's first integrated steel plant come tumbling down? In November 1924, it appeared that Tata Steel was on the verge of closing down.

But Dorabji Tata was a man inspired by the ideals and principles of his father. To him, paying the employees their wages took precedence over everything else because it was livelihoods at stake. He knew that he had to save the company so that it could survive these very difficult times. At that point he took a step that has gone down in the history of the company as the act that saved Tata Steel.

His wife and he decided to pledge their entire personal wealth, which came to around Rs 1 crore, to raise funds for Tata Steel. This included all the jewellery owned by his wife, including the famed Jubilee Diamond. This fabulous diamond, weighing 245.35 carats, was twice as large as the legendary Kohinoor and had been gifted by Dorabji to his beloved wife Meherbai many years earlier.

Against Dorabji's pledge of his personal wealth, the Imperial Bank of India provided the Tatas with a loan of Rs 1 crore. This money was used to pay the wages of the workers at Tata Steel and also to fund the company for the short term. Thanks to this, production of steel at Jamshedpur continued without any significant interruption. The company's greatest crisis had been averted, and Tata Steel survived.

Dorabji had done what he thought was right. It did not matter to him that he was using his personal wealth to rescue a company that was owned by a firm (Tata Sons) and several other shareholders. What did matter greatly to him was doing the right thing.

In addition to the funds raised through Dorabji's pledge of his personal wealth, the company also borrowed money from Gwalior State to keep Tata Steel running. Every employee was paid on time and not a single worker was laid off during the crisis of 1924. On the other hand, shareholders were not paid dividends for the next several years until the company had fully recovered. The funds that became available were instead used to complete the large expansion programme envisioned earlier, because Dorabji, R.D. Tata and other directors of Tata Steel believed that this would yield the best long-term benefits for the company. They were quite correct in pursuing this path because the expanded capacity benefited the company hugely by the 1930s, by which time the demand for steel revived and then went up significantly.

Tata Steel had not merely survived, it prospered hugely in the decades ahead. Today it is one of the finest steel companies in the world. If you are ever in Jamshedpur, please take some time to visit the beautifully laid out Dorabji Tata Park there. In this park you will see a huge steel replica of the Jubilee Diamond. This replica was designed and installed by the company a few years ago, as a tribute to Dorabji Tata and his wife Meherbai, who saved Tata Steel from collapse with this diamond and with their hearts of gold.

* * *

2. The Dilemmas of J.R.D. Tata

The principles that matter to leaders are perhaps tested most severely when they face dilemmas of an ethical nature. Here are two stories from the life of J.R.D. Tata, which reflect this truth.

In both these stories you will see the mind of J.R.D. Tata hard at work as he endeavours to pursue the 'sound and straightforward business principles' that Jamsetji Tata had described as the bedrock on which the Tata Group had been founded.

The first story concerns Tata Airlines (which was later renamed Air India). J.R.D. Tata had co-founded this airline in 1932, along with a British aviator called Neville Vintcent. In fact, it was Vintcent who had first put forward to JRD, in 1929, a proposal for starting a commercial airline in India. JRD had taken to this idea enthusiastically. Later, Vintcent also worked closely with JRD in setting up the aviation operations of the Tata Group and in making Tata Airlines one of the best-managed and most punctual airlines in the whole of the British empire.

At the start of the enterprise, in 1932, Vintcent had been promised one-third of the profits of the airline, for his entrepreneurial contribution and leadership of the venture. J.R.D. Tata's services and the financial investment required for the venture came from the Tata Group, which owned the airline. This commercial arrangement continued unchanged for the next five years. By 1937, Tata Airlines was a much larger enterprise than it had been at the start. Profits, which had been at Rs 60,000 in the first year of operations, were now ten times more. As a result, Vintcent's remuneration had also increased tenfold.

Vintcent's original contract expired at the end of five years, in 1937, and it was now time to renew the arrangement. At this point, J.D. Choksi, a fine legal mind and respected solicitor, advised JRD and his fellow directors that the contract should not be renewed on the same terms since the profits were much larger now. This would also ensure that Vintcent's remuneration stayed within reasonable boundaries. The directors agreed with this advice. J.R.D. Tata was unhappy, but went along with this decision. At that time JRD was not yet the chairman of the Tata Group. He would assume that role only a year later, in 1938.

What happened thereafter has been narrated by J.R.D. Tata to his biographer R.M. Lala. JRD says that when he suggested to Neville Vintcent that a new and revised arrangement would have to be discussed, Vintcent responded by saying that 'an agreement is an agreement' and it would need to be honoured. In other words, he clearly wanted the initial arrangement of getting one-third of the profits to stay in place. If this was not done, Vintcent would offer to quit.

By that time Tata Airlines was a large-enough organization to do without Vintcent and had many competent officers manning its operations. Vintcent's presence was important, but it was no longer essential. JRD could perhaps easily have dispensed with Vintcent's presence in the airline and saved a lot of money too.

But JRD began agonizing over the matter. His mind was not at peace with the decision. Deep within, he perhaps thought that what was being proposed was unfair to Vintcent, without whom the airline would never have been created in the first place. He now went to another respected solicitor in Mumbai, a man named Dinshaw Daji, who often advised JRD on his personal matters.

JRD briefed Dinshaw Daji on the situation and also told him that he wanted to do the right thing. Daji considered the facts of the case, twisted the *feta* (Parsi hat) that sat on his head, and told JRD that Choksi's proposal of entering into a revised arrangement in the new contract was legally correct. However, morally, Vintcent was entitled to the share that he had been promised.

JRD pondered on Daji's advice and decided to do what was morally right rather than what was only legally correct. He went to Neville Vintcent and assured him that the terms of his contract would continue to remain unchanged. Vintcent continued to work with Tata Airlines, though he tragically passed away a few years later.

JRD also mentions to his biographer that he was very firm with his colleagues in a memo that he sent out to them explaining his stance on continuing with Vintcent's existing terms. However, since the Tata Group had always respected the moral aspects of conducting business, he was confident that they would agree. In fact, this was indeed the case, and none of his colleagues said no to his decision.

In retrospect, JRD felt that he had permitted a situation to be created where the proposed revised arrangements were unfair to his senior colleague Vintcent. He also felt disappointed that he had not stood up for what he believed was fair and right when the original discussion on this subject with Choksi had happened. However, the dilemma at hand had been resolved.

The second story occurs over four decades later, in the 1980s, by which time J.R.D. Tata was not just long-serving chairman of the Tata Group but also a patriarch of Indian industry. It concerns the small but interesting matter of a pen that he once lost.

This personal story has been narrated by Dr J.J. Irani, a senior director of the Tata Group who led Tata Steel for many years. 'Doc. Irani', as he is popularly called, had the opportunity to interact with JRD on many occasions.

JRD and the senior Tata directors used to meet for lunch on the fourth floor of Bombay House, the Tata Group's headquarters, every day. The lunch table was also the venue for many informal conversations.

One day, JRD came to lunch, sad that he had lost his favourite pen. He used to always carry a Parker pen set—a fountain pen and a ball pen.

'Look,' he said sadly, 'I have lost the ball pen. I don't know where it has gone. I have looked all over . . . but it's gone.'

One of the directors in the lunch room that day was Doc. Irani. He made note of J.R.D. Tata's loss. A few weeks later, when he was visiting London, he went to a small shop near Selfridge's specializing in pens and found a ball pen identical to the one JRD had lost. He bought it immediately. The next time he met J.R.D. Tata, he presented that pen to him.

JRD was delighted. 'Yes, Jamshed, it is exactly like the one I lost.' JRD tried it out for one or two minutes. Then Dr Irani saw JRD's expression change slowly. After a couple of minutes, he gave the ball pen back to Dr Irani, and said, 'Thank you for the thought. This is exactly what I wanted, but I cannot accept it.'

'Why?' asked Dr Irani, 'I thought you were looking for this.'

JRD answered, 'Yes, Jamshed. But it is a principle of mine not to accept any gifts from any of my colleagues at work. If I did, then I know my colleagues would try to outdo each other and give me exorbitant gifts.'

Dr Irani tried to persuade him to accept the pen. 'But Sir, nobody would know that I have given you this pen. You can say that you found it in your room. I am not going to go around saying that I have given JRD an identical pen.'

JRD responded, 'Jamshed, I know you will not do any such thing. But I would know. I would know that I accepted this gift against my principles. I am sorry, but I cannot accept it.'

Each of us decides the principles by which we lead our lives, the principles that we will stand by even if no one is looking or speaking about them. These principles define who we really are. While this specific story concerns only the small matter of a lost pen, it reflects the kind of principles that would have inevitably guided so many other aspects of J.R.D. Tata's decision-making throughout his long and distinguished career as chairman of the Tata Group.

* * *

3. Tata Finance Runs into Trouble

In April 2001, a letter written by a person who called himself Shankar Sharma reached the offices of many top officials of the Tata Group. The recipients of the letter included the directors of Tata Finance Limited, India's stock market regulator, the Securities and Exchange Board of India (SEBI) and several leading newspapers.

The letter levelled serious allegations against Tata Finance and its erstwhile managing director Dilip Pendse. It charged the company with publishing falsified information in its prospectus for a rights issue of preference shares. It also alleged that a large fraud had been committed in the company.

Tata Finance Limited was a company with big ambitions. At that time it was the Tata Group's flagship platform for growth in the financial services industry. It had built a good presence in several areas, including hire and purchase of commercial vehicles, and financing of cars and consumer durables. The company accepted fixed deposits from the public, offering a good rate of interest. Tens of thousands of Indians had invested their life savings with Tata Finance, primarily driven by their trust in the Tata name. Dilip Pendse, the managing director, was the chief architect of many of these plans and was considered a financial whiz kid in many circles.

The letter from Shankar Sharma therefore came as a rude shock to the Tata top brass. An audit of Tata Finance was carried out immediately, to ascertain whether there was any truth in the allegations. Ishaat Hussain, who was the finance director at Tata Sons at that time, says, 'That letter alerted us, and further investigations revealed that there had indeed been some serious irregularities. We were all taken aback.'

The investigations threw up some painfully clear facts. Because of some dubious investments by the management, the company had become almost insolvent. It had significant borrowings, of about Rs 2,700 crore. Of this, Rs 875 crore represented money belonging to 4 lakh small depositors. For many of them these were savings of a lifetime, funds kept aside for retirement, children's marriages and medical emergencies. Now Tata Finance was not in a position to repay these depositors.

The cause of this crisis also soon became clear. Tata Finance, led by Dilip Pendse, had lent approximately Rs 525 crore to some of its own subsidiary companies and affiliates, including a company called Nishkalp. A large part of that money had been invested in the equity market, in scrips of poor and speculative quality. In fact, some of these transactions had been carried out to earn personal profits. When the value of these scrips crashed, the original investments vanished, leading to a gaping hole in the books of the company.

This was a moment of reckoning for the Tatas, a group which was considered the gold standard for integrity in the country. How would they deal with a fraud of this magnitude?

The response to this crisis was steered by Ratan Tata, chairman of Tata Sons, himself. He led from the front. The matter was discussed with the board of Tata Sons, the parent company of the group. Ishaat Hussain recalls, 'Mr Tata recommended to the Tata Sons board that they stand behind the Company and make available funds to meet all its financial commitments, and the Board fully endorsed this.'

The quantum of money involved—over Rs 500 crore—was a very large sum at that time. Meeting this entire liability created by the fraud exceeded the limited legal responsibilities of Tata Sons, because Tata Finance had many other shareholders as well. Tata Sons was indeed the promoter shareholder, but its liability was limited, as laid out under the law.

This did not constrain the response of Ratan Tata and the leadership at Tata Sons, because they were clearly focused on what was morally right to do rather than what was legally necessary. In fact, Ratan Tata defined two clear principles that would guide the Tata Group's response to the crisis.

First, the interests of every depositor would be fully protected so that no one who had trusted the Tata name lost on account of the wrong actions of the management of Tata Finance. To do this, Tata Sons would make available the necessary funds, as approved by its board of directors.

Second, a thorough investigation would be undertaken so that the people who were guilty could be pursued legally and punished for their actions, regardless of how senior or well-connected they were.

Both these actions were implemented swiftly. On 25 July 2001, an extraordinary public statement was issued admitting that Tata Finance was in distress because of a fraud committed upon it. This statement went on to say that the Tatas would ensure that no depositor in the company lost any money.

To ensure this, the holding company of the Tata Group, Tata Sons, and its sister company Tata Industries, quickly provided Tata Finance with cash and corporate guarantees amounting to Rs 615 crore so that funds would be available to repay each and every investor, as and when required. It was of paramount importance that every investor should feel safe and sleep peacefully.

In addition, plans were put in place to ensure that every depositor who wanted his money back was repaid immediately, at every branch of the company across India.

As you read this, do bear in mind that in 2001, electronic fund transfers and digital money were not yet in vogue. Tata Finance actually kept a helicopter on standby so that funds could be transported urgently by air, if necessary.

Fortunately, this helicopter was not used at all because people trusted the assurance provided by the Tata Group that their funds were safe. Only a handful of the 4 lakh small depositors withdrew their money. One of the authors (Harish) had a fixed deposit in Tata Finance in those days, and the thought of withdrawing it did not even cross his mind because he had seen the statement issued by the Tata Group and instinctively felt his money would be absolutely safe.

The second track of action, as outlined by Ratan Tata—that of pursuing the guilty—was also taken forward immediately. The finance and legal heads at Tata Sons executed the actions required here with precision and speed.

To begin with, an internal team, supplemented with external auditors, assessed all the documents available and built up a paper trail. By the first week of August, based on expert legal and accounting advice, Tata Finance and Tata Industries filed a first information report with the economic offences wing of Mumbai Police against Pendse and certain other former Tata Finance employees.

The Tata Group was unrelenting in its resolve to bring the culprits to book. This was not just to ensure that the guilty were punished but also to send a clear message about how the Group viewed any deviations from its value systems and code of integrity, regardless of how senior or well regarded the people concerned were.

Ishaat Hussain has written about this:

> We moved the courts when the Mumbai police filed
> a closure report with respect to our complaints. We
> took that stance that we will not let go the culprits. We
> moved the Bombay High Court and got the investigation
> transferred to the Central Bureau of Investigation. In
> the Supreme Court, too, our stand was vindicated. Six
> criminal complaints were filed in all, including three
> with the Delhi police, and six complaints with SEBI for
> violation of various securities laws. Dilip Pendse was
> charge-sheeted in two complaints, and was taken into
> judicial custody.

Even as these actions progressed in the courts of law, the
Tata Group reflected on the shortcomings that had led
to the lapses at Tata Finance. Clearly, some checks and
balances had failed, and there had been shortcomings in key
areas of corporate governance. A thorough understanding
of the root causes was established. This led to the Group
putting in place several processes to strengthen systems of
governance across all its companies. Some of these were
required by statute, and others were crafted specifically as
policies of the Tata Group.

Two things stand out from this story. First, things
had indeed gone wrong in Tata Finance. Second, the Tata
Group's transparent, principled handling of this crisis
brought to the fore the essential character and some of the
key values of the Group.

As one of the authors (Gopal) has said, referring to
this crisis:

It takes a lot of trust to be appointed as a leader. I see greatness of character in this admission that once in a while things will and do go wrong. Don't push them under the carpet. Deal with them. Very few large Corporations in India do this in practice.

8

Profits

'The whole of that wealth is held in trust for the people and used exclusively for their benefit. The cycle is thus complete; what came from the people has gone back to the people many times over'—J.R.D. Tata, in his foreword to the book *Jamsetji Nusserwanji Tata: A Chronicle of His Life* by Frank Harris.

The 'P' considered in this chapter being 'profit', it must be appreciated that this is among the most misunderstood of terms when it comes to business. For some it is the very purpose of an enterprise; for yet others it is a key purpose, though not the only purpose; for some others it is not the purpose but merely the by-product of enterprise, a sort of metric to demonstrate the positive effect of business. We have participated in discussions that range from 'what else is the purpose of a business other than profits' to 'money is what makes the world go around'.

Accompanying this essay are three examples from the Tatas, in the context of profits, over the decades.

The first narrates the approach taken by the founder when he established a start-up called Empress Mills. In its early years it was no different from any start-up of today, just as a baby in those days was no different from a baby of today. But the story of its establishment exemplifies the breadth of conceptualization the founder was capable of. In the common aspects of the project, his involvement was deep, whether it was in purchase of the land, erection of the factory, experimentation with new technology and the running of the unit. But he also thought of many uncommon details in running the establishment, installing ventilation for the comfort of the workers, khus-khus curtains for cooling the outside ambient hot air and designing an accident-compensation scheme and a pension scheme for the workers. Empress Mills became one of the most profitable enterprises of its time, but Jamsetji ensured that part of the profits was consistently used for these worker welfare measures.

The second story is of the period from the 1980s onwards, when the Tatas bought into a company that later was christened Tata Coffee Ltd. The leadership of the company had its hands full trying to learn and implement all they could about the coffee bush, its tending and nurturing, and the processing of the coffee beans to meet consumer tastes. Yet the unit demanded of the management something as unusual as an understanding of elephants. Elephants born on and living in the vicinity of the company's estates posed some danger to the families of the workers, and there was the constant threat of man-animal conflict that was good for neither man nor animal. The company therefore employed an 'elephant expert' to guide its response, implemented a host of other unconventional actions and succeeded to a great degree in containing the potential man-animal conflict. As a result, both the workers and the elephants live in relative peace today. It thus demonstrated how profits could be used effectively and innovatively to ensure safety of the workers and also protect the natural ecosystem in which the business operates.

The third narrative is from contemporary times. There was no expert on the COVID pandemic when it struck us towards end-2019. The threat to employees, vendors, allies and society at large was terrifying, as most readers would know, having survived those recent years. Due to the consumer responses during the pandemic and big changes in their buying patterns, there was a lot of business uncertainty for many months, company volumes suffered and so did profits. Notwithstanding this, the Tata Trusts and companies of the Group pledged a substantial sum of money to mitigate the ravages of the pandemic. The details appear in the narrative.

The common feature in the three examples is that the Tata leaders were thinking about matters that would normally not have been key subjects of leadership consideration at the time. In times of stress—relating to a start-up, a new acquisition or a health threat—company leaders tend to think of cost control and cash conservation. In addition, many companies tend to think of maximizing profits as the key objective of the corporation. Though having the same profit motive as any entrepreneur, the Tatas repeatedly did something contrarian. Why? What is the Tata philosophy regarding profits?

For sure there are multiple views on profits, none of them wholly wrong, though none wholly correct either. Profit is a good thing, but perhaps in some proportion only. Profit is indeed the oxygen of a business. Without profits, a business will suffocate, just as without oxygen human life will be snuffed out. But can a human being have too much of oxygen?

Humans breathe to get oxygen, which is present in the air to the extent of 21 per cent. Inert nitrogen comprises 78 per cent of the atmospheric air, which is breathed in and out unchanged by humans. Trace gases make up the final 1 per cent. If a human can live in an environment of pure oxygen, is it healthy? My medical friends tell me that excess of oxygen 'will overwhelm the blood, disrupt the central nervous system and damage the lungs, heart and brain'.

Profits and growth are the oxygen of business. Is it possible to get 'too much' and damage the enterprise irreparably? Just as the 78 per cent of nitrogen in the air is essential for human well-being, immutable values must always accompany profits. It is important to appreciate that a surfeit of profits and wealth is damaging. It is essential to design an enterprise for profits to be always accompanied by values, like air which has both oxygen and nitrogen.

Applied to enterprise leadership, Vedantic philosophies adumbrate four principles: self-awareness, protection of the resources that facilitate one's business, service of others before service of oneself and execution of firm decisions but with compassion. These four apparently simple and ancient concepts cover all our contemporary mumbo-jumbo: compassion, stakeholders, sustainability, humanism . . . you name it. The more modern way of expressing this would be to say, 'harness innovation for public good, put people at the centre, spread economic opportunity, engage in new alliances, be performance-driven in everything, practice superior governance and pursue purpose beyond profits'.

A prosaic debate often arises, as to whether more profits and more growth are valid ends in themselves. Perhaps not, unless the actions are circumscribed by values and purpose. The most powerful people in business pose a conundrum to observers. They seem to take some actions that smack of greed, avarice and narcissism on the one hand, but some also perform great acts of merchant charity for the benefit of society at large, on the other. How can these contradictory deeds be reconciled? Society is never sure how to regard powerful business barons.

The truth may well lie in the fact that such leaders—very rare and few, by the way—view the world though different lenses from ours. What they see is not what others see. The author Richard Tedlow, who has studied such geniuses, has observed, 'There was something special, a bright beam of light which illuminated a previously unseen landscape. What these people realized was that the changes they could make or that others were making was their friend, not their enemy.'[1]

Truth be told, too many entrepreneurs fancy themselves as being such geniuses. There is an insatiable hunger in them for profits, an element of delusion that convinces them that if they acted as some well-established wealthy folks did, then they would prove their genius—a tautological improbability. This delusion leads to hubristic behaviour; they begin to live in their own echo chambers, not listening to others, becoming pompous and boastful, and developing an inability to distinguish between customer focus and hyper-competitiveness. Such was the story of the junk bond trader Michael Milken in the 1980s. He may not have intended to do what he did, but he crossed what Indians recognize as the *Lakshman rekha*. Then it became too late for Milken to avoid jail.

When an economic environment makes it possible for a chosen few to make disproportionate amounts of money and wealth, the tendency arises among too many others, some deserving and some not, to enter the echo chamber of delusion. The industrial revolution unleashed this phenomenon, notably in the United States, and later in Europe. And now it is all over the world. Inequality of an unacceptable level grows until at some imprecise stage society responds, often through a violent revolution. Think about the French and the Russian revolutions.

Readers may be familiar with the predictions of the Indian American economist Professor Ravi Batra of Southern Methodist University, USA. His well-commented-on New York Times bestseller, *The Great Depression of 1990*, predicted a crash of the global economy in 1990.[2]

As the three narratives suggest, in its own idiosyncratic manner the Tata Group adopted a set of ideas and practices from the founder, which have helped it get a mindset that places it among the world's few 'socialist capitalists'. The stories that follow will help you appreciate why Jamsetji Tata still matters to Tata, and perhaps to several other firms in the country.

Stories of Profits

1. The Story of Empress Mills

The first major greenfield industrial venture established by Jamsetji Tata was the Central India Spinning, Weaving and Manufacturing Company Limited, at Nagpur. It was popularly referred to as Empress Mills. It was one of the most profitable enterprises of its time in India. However, what made it a truly outstanding endeavour was the deep sense of responsibility it had towards its workers and the community, which accompanied the earning of these profits.

Jamsetji Tata founded Empress Mills in 1874. He believed that producing goods of the highest quality was the road to sustained success, and hence focused on the use of long-staple cotton in these mills. In addition, he quickly invested in technological innovations, such as the ring spindle, which substantially improved the output of the factory. In the initial years, Jamsetji involved himself deeply in the purchase of land for the factory, and its erection and choice of machinery, experimenting with new technology and putting in place the required manpower. In later years, he delegated the operations of the unit to an excellent and trustworthy manager, Bezonji Dadabhai Mehta, who ran the mills with great dedication and consistent efficiency.

On the back of this well-thought-out strategy, based on superior quality, high productivity and good leadership, Empress Mills soon became a very profitable company. The Mills had begun with a capital of only Rs 15 lakh. However, between 1886 and 1899, the capital was twice increased and the profits were so handsome that every shareholder received a number of bonus shares. By 1913, the earnings exceeded thirteen times the original capital and a share of face value of Rs 500 was already worth Rs 5,718. By June 1920, the total profits of the Empress Mills had exceeded Rs 7 crore, a huge amount at that time, and nearly fifty times the original capital. Jamsetji Tata's ambition was for Empress Mills to pay dividends of 100 per cent each year, and in 1920, Mills more than fulfilled his dream by paying a dividend of 160 per cent. The shareholders were thus exceedingly well rewarded, and Jamsetji was seen as an astute businessman and a bold pioneer of the cotton industry in India.

What made Empress Mills truly special was not the scale or rapid increase of its profits but the responsibility with which they were earned and used. To begin with, Jamsetji Tata went about improving the conditions of factory life for his workers. He gave great care to ensure that the air in the factory was fresh for the workers within, to protect their health. In fact, Empress Mills was the first factory in India where ventilation was accorded the highest priority. Jamsetji also experimented with new and better methods of ventilation. Speaking in 1895, he described one such experiment which was just about to begin:

We have paid the greatest attention to sanitary
arrangements . . . we have provided fans for ventilation,
humidifiers to prevent the effects of extremely dry air,
khus-khus tatties for cooling the rooms, which must, by
the nature of our business, get hotter in the hot weather.
But still we are not quite satisfied with what we have
done. We are about to start a new scheme in the shed . . .
this scheme, we hope, will be a great improvement upon
what we have already done and we are confident that
if it succeeds in nothing else, it is sure to succeed in one
thing, and that is in giving an equally distributed supply
of free, fresh and pure air to our workpeople.

It is fascinating to note how much time and attention
Jamsetji Tata was personally investing in this subject,
because he believed it was important for the welfare of his
workers. But he went beyond this too.

In 1887, Jamsetji Tata introduced a gratuitous pension
fund for the workers of these Mills. This was the first
of its kind in the country. In 1895, he introduced an
accident compensation scheme for his workers. In 1901,
he introduced a Provident Fund scheme for his workers.
Once again, this was the first time ever in India that this
concept had been introduced. Each of these pioneering
worker welfare schemes cost significant sums of money,
and many people may even have considered them wasteful
or unnecessary. However, Jamsetji felt that the welfare
of the workers and these schemes for their benefit were a
primary responsibility of the management.

At Empress Mills, such care for the workers and the
community, notwithstanding the costs involved, soon

became a way of life. Seven night schools were established, where workers were taught languages, music and dance. Women and girls were provided classes where they were taught elementary skills such as reading, writing and needlework. Four gymnasia were established to give ample opportunity to the workers for physical exercise.

For women, a maternity benefit allowance was put in place in 1921. Women who had been employed for eleven months or more were provided two months' paid maternity benefit. Two well-appointed creches were set up for the babies of women employed at the Mills. It is amazing to reflect on the fact that all this happened over a century ago.

In addition, women's education in the wider community was a particular area of focus. The Empress Mills and its directors provided a generous grant for the establishment of a girls' high school in Nagpur, in 1921, the Jamsetji Tata Girls' High School, in tribute to the founder, who had passed away some years ago. An endowment was created to ensure that this school would obtain a regular annual income.

One of the authors (Harish) visited this school in 2023, over 100 years after it had been founded. He found it to be a flourishing and vibrant institution, very well-regarded in the city. Right in front of the impressive school building stands a statue of Jamsetji Tata, holding in his hands a small replica of Empress Mills, where his philosophy of 'profits with responsibility' had unfolded and evolved.

Jamsetji Tata also used the learnings from his accomplishments at Empress Mills to encourage the cultivation of Egyptian cotton of a finer class of staple in India. In his view, this was essential for the country to compete successfully against Japan and the European nations. He published a memorandum on the subject in 1896, urging his countrymen to consider how India's 'young and only industry' could be saved from destruction. The cultivation of Egyptian cotton in the country was an ambitious plan, and initial efforts did not yield consistent results. Unfortunately, Jamsetji Tata passed away in 1904, before this subject could be addressed fully. However, in triggering discussion on this subject, Jamsetji also made an important point—that a profitable company has a larger responsibility to the industry that it is part of, and to the nation at large.

2. A Truly Good Cup of Coffee

Tata Coffee is India's leading integrated coffee plantation company. It has a proud heritage of more than 100 years, and was acquired by the Tata Group in 1990. The company's lush green estates are located in the southern part of India, primarily in the fertile Coorg region, which is blessed by the beautiful Cauvery river. Tata Coffee makes fine arabica and robusta coffees, which are marketed in India and also supplied to some of the best coffee roasters across the world.

Over the past several years, the company has successfully focused on profitable growth and on becoming a proud flag-bearer for Indian coffees worldwide. To drive these business objectives, it has perfected the art of producing specialty coffees, including microlots, which have unique taste and flavour characteristics and therefore earn a premium from coffee connoisseurs. The company has also set itself on a persistent quest for excellence and quality in all the coffees it produces, quite similar to the journey that Jamsetji Tata undertook in a very different industry (textiles) at Empress Mills over a century ago. As a result of these and other initiatives, Tata Coffee has consistently delivered good financial results.

However, around 2015, the company faced a unique and urgent problem, which had nothing to do with coffee and profits and everything to do with elephants and people. There were increasing incidents of conflict between elephants and humans on its plantations. Congregations of elephants would gather in the forests of Coorg and often stray into the coffee estates in search of food and water. They included over forty elephants that had been born in that area over the past twenty-five years. The appearance of these elephants on the plantations often caused panic amongst the workers, and there would also be damage to the crops.

The leadership of Tata Coffee decided to address this matter on top priority, because they believed that the company had a responsibility towards the safety of its people, and also towards providing the elephants a harmonious environment to live in. One of the authors (Harish) was, at that time, the chairman of the board of directors of Tata Coffee. He recalls that this subject was tabled by the management at more than one board meeting and discussed at length. The conclusion: notwithstanding the costs, this issue needed urgent and sustainable resolution.

We are unaware of other instances of corporate boards devoting lengthy meetings to discussing elephants in such detail. Yet this was viewed as one of the most important tasks at that time, because Tata Coffee had always believed that protecting and nurturing a healthy environment and ecosystem was at the foundation of its business of producing 'good coffee'.

The managing director of the company (Sanjiv Sarin, and thereafter his successor Chacko Thomas) personally led this initiative, emphasizing its importance. Chacko Thomas recalls that they initially reached out to an elephant expert based in Kochi. This expert recommended that the company recruit a full-time expert in elephant behaviour who could help formulate the response to the issue. This led to the appointment of Karthik Krishna, who joined Tata Coffee to set up and lead the wildlife cell. Karthik also established a dedicated elephant-tracking team in the company.

The wildlife cell studied the migration patterns of the elephants and the corridors they traversed when they entered the coffee plantations. They understood that the elephants left their forest habitat in search of water, because climate change had made water scarce in the forests, particularly during some periods during the year. So the company constructed water bodies in the areas outside the plantations so the elephants could drink their fill of water without having to enter the human habitations on the estates.

The team understood that the elephants also came in search of jackfruit, the smell of which would often make them go berserk. So the fruits on the jackfruit trees in the premises of the coffee plantations were cut down before they matured to remove this source of temptation altogether.

Very importantly, the corridors used by elephants across the estates were mapped in great detail using GIS polygons. A cadre of full-time elephant trackers was trained to track, monitor and report elephant movements. At its peak, this team consisted of 170 people, spread across all the coffee plantations. In addition, in conjunction with the Forest Department of Karnataka, the matriarch elephants were radio-collared, as the herd tended to follow its matriarch, making tracking easy. Early-warning SMSes (on mobile phones) would go out to people inhabiting any specific area around which elephants were sighted. This would ensure that sudden and unfortunate encounters were completely avoided.

Using the detailed insights available on elephant behaviour, the workers on the plantation were regularly trained on how to respond if one of the majestic beasts were to cross their path unexpectedly. In many instances, maintaining calm and staying one's ground rather than running helter-skelter in panic was the right way to ensure that one did not agitate the elephant. Such training had to be carried out in several languages since there were many migrant workers on the estates from different parts of the country.

Finally, a few rogue or troublesome elephants were relocated safely to elephant reserves. All these steps were undertaken in collaboration with the state government of Karnataka and its Forest Department.

As a result of all these initiatives, the plantation workers of Tata Coffee feel safe in their estates. Equally importantly, the elephants are happier as well, because, like most animals, they too wish to live in peace and harmony.

Perhaps when you have your next cup of Tata Coffee, you can imagine their gleaming tusks and smiles reflected in your steaming cup.

This sense of deep and whole-hearted responsibility to its community and environment has been Tata Coffee's way of life for a long time, and certainly ever since the company became part of the Tata Group. In 1990, the acquisition of this company, through a first-of-its-kind open offer, had been led by the Tata veteran Darbari Seth. Immediately afterwards, one of the very first major announcements that Seth made was not about business strategy or vision but on the establishment of the Coorg Foundation. This foundation was set up with a significant endowment, specifically to contribute to the well-being of the community in Coorg.

Over the past three decades, the Coorg Foundation has led the way in many community initiatives. For instance, the Swastha Centre for Special Education and Rehabilitation was established in 2003 to take care of differently-abled children from the local communities. It houses children who belong to needy families from the surrounding areas, providing them boarding and lodging. It works towards developing their physical and mental attributes, and trains them to become productive. These children learn valuable skills, such as screen-printing, book-binding, tailoring and paper-bag making, which enhances their employability as well. Since its inception, several thousand students have benefited through the initiatives of Swastha.

Tata Coffee has also invested significantly in helping the tribal communities of the area through free medical care and emergency aid. The company provides continuous support to the Rural India Health Project (RIHP) Hospital located in Coorg. In a very different space, the Tata Coffee Hornbill Foundation creates awareness about the great Indian hornbill, an endangered bird, and also helps protect its natural habitat, including the trees that these birds use for their nesting and roosting. The company has also implemented a host of other environment-focused initiatives, including rainwater harvesting on a large scale.

Sustained growth and profits are very important to safeguarding the future of Tata Coffee. This requires complete commitment to quality, productivity, execution and product innovation, and the capability to serve customer needs outstandingly well. But at the heart of the company's journey is its desire and commitment to doing business with full responsibility towards its community and its environment. That is what goes into a truly good and delicious cup of coffee.

3. The Fight Against COVID-19

In early 2020, the COVID-19 pandemic stopped the world in its tracks. Initial news reports highlighted tens of thousands of deaths and millions of people falling ill with the virus, which had begun wreaking havoc in its very first wave of infections. On 25 March 2020, the prime minister of India announced a national lockdown for twenty-one days, in an effort to contain the spread of the deadly pandemic. Schools, colleges and non-essential commercial establishments all shut down.

This was an unanticipated emergency, and corporations, including the Tata Group, contemplated an uncertain future even as their factories, retail stores and offices shut down. It was unclear when these would reopen. Given the significant fixed costs of these establishments, cash losses began mounting by the day.

Within three days of commencement of the national lockdown, the leadership of the Tata Group had formulated its first response. On 28 March 2020, statements were issued by Ratan Tata, chairman of the Tata Trusts, and N. Chandrasekaran, chairman of Tata Sons, committing a very significant total amount of Rs 1,500 crore to the fight against COVID-19.

Ratan Tata's statement said:

The current situation in India and across the world is of grave concern and needs immediate action . . . Tata Trusts and the Tata group's companies have in the past risen to the needs of the nation . . . Today, Tata Trusts continue their pledge to protect and empower all affected communities, and is committing Rs. 500 crores . . .

N. Chandrasekaran's statement added:

The current situation in India and other parts of the world owing to the impact of COVID-19 is very worrisome and requires our best action. Tata Sons announces an additional Rs. 1,000 crores support towards COVID-19 and related activities. We will work together with the Tata Trusts and our Chairman Emeritus Mr. Tata and would be fully supporting their initiatives, and work in a collaborative manner to bring (to bear) the full expertise of the Group.

These statements were remarkable yet unexceptional. They were remarkable because, at that specific point in time the future was very uncertain. The profit-making engines of the Group had been impacted significantly and adversely. Yet here was the Tata Group, committing such a large amount from its accumulated profits and reserves to the fight against the pandemic.

However, they were also unexceptional statements because responsible use of its wealth for the community was embedded in the mission of the Tata Group, as defined by its founder Jamsetji Tata. His philosophy of putting the community centre-stage had always guided the group's decision-making.

This commitment of funds for the long fight ahead translated into strong and concerted action on the ground very quickly. At Tata Sons, chairman Chandrasekaran constituted a task force headed by Banmali Agrawala, a key member of his leadership team. One of the authors (Harish) was privileged to be a member of this task force during the second wave of the pandemic. He recalls that the team met online every alternate morning at 8 a.m., without fail, to rigorously chart out the key initiatives for the days ahead. There was a sense of urgency and an overriding feeling of responsibility.

Over the next several months, requests from different states and entities poured in for contributions. The most sought-after critical items were ventilators, personal protective equipment (PPE), testing kits and oxygen. The Tata Group used its expertise and network to provide over 1,500 ventilators and 1.5 million PPE kits for the frontline warriors fighting COVID. During the second wave of the pandemic, when oxygen was in very high demand, around 10 per cent of India's oxygen requirements came from the factories of the Tata Group.

The Tata Group also contributed to the creation of more than 5,000 new hospital beds across the country for use by patients fighting the COVID-19 virus. This included some greenfield hospitals too. One such establishment was a 551-bed COVID hospital that came up at Kasaragod in Kerala state, funded by Tata Sons, designed and built from the ground up in 100 days by a passionate team from Tata Projects. The project was ably supported by other Tata companies in their respective areas of expertise. Modular steel units were provided by Tata Steel. Voltas provided the air-conditioning and Tata Consulting Engineers designed the modular pre-fabricated units. The hospital was then handed over to the local administration in record time.

Simultaneously, businesses of the Tata Group adapted swiftly to the demands of the pandemic, working tirelessly to provide their customers essential products and services while ensuring the highest levels of safety for their workers. For example, Tata Power ensured that their seventy renewable power plants, eleven thermal and hydro-generation plants, along with their transmission and distribution networks, operated diligently through the pandemic to provide uninterrupted electricity to its millions of customers. Tata Consultancy Services worked with their customers across the globe to provide the required technology support. Tata Consumer Products quickly rejigged its logistics and supply chain to ensure that essential everyday products such as Tata Tea and Tata Salt were available to their customers nationwide.

There was equal attention paid to the needs of employees of the Group, who were, like everyone else, badly shaken by the pandemic. Safeguarding jobs was a key area of focus. The health and safety of employees were accorded the highest priority. Later, once COVID-19 vaccines had been developed and approved by the government, Tata companies also ran vaccination camps for all their employees and encouraged them to get vaccinated promptly. A Group-wide communication campaign with the catchy Hinglish tagline 'Vaccine Lo, Let's go!' urged employees and their families to get vaccinated immediately. The entire effort delivered excellent results.

Even as the group invested significant resources and efforts in the fight against the pandemic, the Tata leadership also utilized this period to strategically review the geopolitical and economic challenges thrown up by this unanticipated global event and cast a thoughtful eye on the industry and how it could serve the key national priorities of the future. Many ideas appear to have emerged from these strategic reviews.

One example is the Tata Group's decision to create a large electronics and semi-conductor design and manufacturing hub in India, under the overall umbrella of Tata Electronics. This appears to have been triggered by the spectre of shifting global supply chains, which came into sharp focus during the pandemic. Countries worldwide looked to diversify their concentrated supply bases for these critical technology products. This was a unique opportunity for India. The Tata Group decided to step in to contribute to this national need—much the way Jamsetji Tata had in the 1890s, when he had resolved to create India's first integrated steel plant because steel was, in his view, a key priority for national progress.

From the 1890s to the 2020s, that core mission, established by Jamsetji Tata, has never changed. The Tata Group has been and continues to be committed to participating in nation-building through industry. The economic wealth generated from such endeavours is then utilized responsibly to serve the needs of the community and the planet—during both good and bad times, including unusually difficult periods, such as the COVID-19 pandemic.

9

Perspectives

Based on historical facts, we imagine a panel discussion among the four former chairmen who led the Tata Group from 1868 to 1991. They are founder Jamsetji Tata, his son Dorabji Tata, Dorabji's successor Nowroji Saklatwala, and the next chairman, J.R.D. Tata.[1]

Jamsetji: *Aao dikra.* It has been a long time since we chatted together. The company we had served has renewed itself constantly to survive and grow. The culture and values of Tata, which have endured for over a century, are very precious. Future leaders must know what aspects of culture must not change and what aspects must adapt to change. However, I suggest a word of caution for our discussion—that we reminisce about our times but do not make judgements about our modern-day successors. They are managing a vastly different business in a vastly different world. Like the three of you, I will always wish and pray that they hold on to the purpose that we had set for the business and some of its core values. I think the Tata companies have done so all of these years.

JRD: Yes, of course, dear Kakaji. As you know, as one of your original partners in the business, my father (RD) would harangue me periodically about your vision and how you had ever so endearingly articulated the purpose of the firm. You had said that the firm is an integral part of the community and that it exists to serve the community. Eighty years later, during the 1960s, when I was the chairman, I said pretty much the same thing in the business language of my times: that what the firm earns from the people must go back to the people, many times over. It is good that this strong foundation and our business purpose have both remained intact, although the profile and appurtenances of the business have changed. There will always be challenging times and apparent aberrations, but I am sure that the true purpose of the firm continues to be what we had intended and articulated it to be, and had practised.

Dorab: It is wonderful to know that our current generation is able to maintain our corporate purpose, that too consistently after more than a century. Among the four of us, we have experienced 150 years of the firm: colonial India, the 1930s Depression, two World Wars, Partition, Independence of our beloved nation, global economic cycles and an explosion in the population of India.

Jamsetji: Yes, that is true, but the intrinsic challenges of running a business surely remained broadly similar to those of our times. I remember what a tough time I had when I bought Dharamsi Mills in Kurla, later renamed as Svadeshi Mills, because the idea of making things in India appealed to me. I was convinced that such acquisitions at a low price must be seriously considered. If I could buy an asset cheap, I felt I had a decent chance to turn it around by making finer products than it did before. Really, it was nerve-racking because the Tata name was at stake. I staked my own wealth and even broke the Trusts to raise the funds required.

Dorab: Papa, you are so right about what happens when the name Tata is at stake. You may recall that you were so indisposed at Bad Neuheim that cousin RD and I came to meet you. You said to us about your wealth, 'If you cannot make it greater, at least preserve it. Do not let things slide. Go on doing my work and increasing it, but if you cannot, do not lose what we have already done.' We could not raise capital from the London market, but Indian financiers surprised us by subscribing to the capital of our steel company. After initial troubles, the company made its first ingot of steel in 1912. Within four years I told shareholders of my plan to expand steel production, as in 1916 I had told them about our bumper earnings due to production being 30 per cent above the designed capacity, our bursting order books and the ready markets! However, the First World War began, transport and labour costs spiralled out of control, and an earthquake struck Japan, the biggest pig iron market. Our steel company was suddenly staring down an abyss.

JRD: Oh yes, Dorabji, my father had told me this story. Was this not the occasion when one of the directors suggested that the government take over the steel mill? My father said he was livid and that he thumped the table, swearing that this would not happen so long as he was alive!

Dorab: Yes indeed, Jeh, your father did. After that episode of thumping the table, we received a telegram from Jamshedpur saying that our money was inadequate to pay the wages of our employees. I went to the Imperial Bank of India and pledged my wife's jewellery to secure a loan. After that, Papa's adopted motto for the firm *Humata, Hukhta, Hvarshta* worked well, because *Ahura Mazda* smiled, and our fortunes turned.

JRD: Yes Dorabji. Even the Taj Mahal hotel, which was one of Kaka's dream projects, took ever so long to make a profit. They used to call it the 'Tata White Elephant'. I found a talented hotelier in Ajit Kerkar, who turned the Taj around brilliantly. During my chairmanship, we acquired a soda ash business at Mithapur. People even told me that we had bought the wrong business in the wrong place. Thanks to the imaginative leadership of another professional, Darbari Seth, the business turned around. I understand that Tata is now the world's second-largest soda ash player.

Saklatwala: Yeah, what you folks say is true; yet there can be exceptions to the situation. You must try very hard to turn around acquisitions or new ventures. But if after trying hard and sincerely, you fail, maybe for market-driven reasons, then you also need to stop the haemorrhage. How long can you persist with operations that you are just unable to turn around? How do you judge when to call it quits? After our time, Tata Textiles and Tata Oil Mills were divested because the Tatas could not see any way to make a sustainable success of them.

Dorab: Indeed you raise a valid issue. I think you have to do everything you possibly can with a great degree of sincerity, and then the time comes to take a call. After 1917 I launched eleven new ventures; in each of them, investors fought to get shares, such was the faith in the Tata name. Apart from Tata Oil Mills, I set up Tata Industrial Bank, New India Assurance Company, Tata Construction, Tata Electro-Chemicals and Tata Sugar Corporation, just to name a few. Market conditions were tough and some of the ventures ran into problems.

Saklatwala: And when I succeeded you, Dorabji, I had to get a grip on the situation I faced. The firm was over-leveraged and the global recession did not help. Your decisions may have been right when you took them, but later developments had their own impact. I expressed my thoughts in a speech, 'Those were truly mad days, and perhaps the maddest feature was the supreme confidence of the public in Tata, and, incidentally, the overconfidence of Tata themselves.' I really felt that these ventures suffered from insufficient preparation before their inception; some of them were over-capitalized in anticipation of rapid expansion, and some from a rapid collapse of market values and prices.

Dorab: Yes, my dear Nowroji, I did hear the stories about those property disposals, but luckily for you, I was not around to express my views! Times have changed, and nowadays businesses are sold and bought, hopefully with grace and fairness. I heard that after the times when we headed the group, the Tata Sons board has periodically debated which businesses should be divested and how. But, to be fair, I did support new businesses too.

Jeh, as I recall, I supported you when you wanted to enter the airline business around 1929.

JRD: Dorabji, in the late 1920s you were totally against my idea of entering the airline business. You felt that we were too stretched at that time, both financially and managerially. The Tata Sons board minutes clearly carried the message of the board rejecting the firm's entry into airlines. So I went to my mentor, John Peterson. You remember him? I cried out my emotions to him.

Dorab: You did put John Peterson on to me. How he pleaded for you. He said something like, 'Let the young man fly with his dreams.' Finally I relented, and you did a great job of developing Tata Airlines. It was one business which you developed personally and could take full credit for. But Jeh, you were ever so keen about the airline. It must have broken your heart to let it go when the government nationalized it.

JRD: In fact, more than nationalization, it was the way I was removed from the chairmanship that hurt me. In business, one must take the decision that is felt to be right, but one must also attempt to implement it gracefully. However, once the government decided to remove me from Air India, I swallowed my pride and accepted it.

Jamsetji: Coming to development of business leaders, Jeh, you referred to Ajit Kerkar and Darbari Seth as great

leaders. I learnt early on that the key to my enterprise would
be to find the right people to run my businesses. I recruited
an extraordinary man called Bezonji Mehta, a self-made
man who had worked in the railways. I trained him and he
responded very well. Later, when I went into steel, I walked
the streets of London and New York to find technocrats.
It was not that I always sought foreign technicians. For
the Taj architecture, I consulted Khanderao Sitaram. Only
after he died did I bring in W.A. Chambers.

JRD: Kakaji, I think you make an exceptional point
about developing technocrats and managers. India had no
business managers in those days, so Tata had to develop
them internally through mentoring as well as by giving them
real-life and hands-on experience. Many Tata leaders went
on to occupy public positions. When India was partitioned,
Prime Minister Liaquat Ali of Pakistan appointed Sir
Ghulam Mohammed, who was a Tata director, as the
new nation's first finance minister. Jawaharlal Nehru,
prime minister of the new Indian government, asked that
Tata director Sir John Mathai join the interim cabinet,
first to be the railway minister, and later to be the second
finance minister in the Union cabinet. A.D. Shroff and
Nani Palkhivala were two stalwarts on the Tata Sons
board who were as influential as finance ministers without
ever becoming finance ministers. When young Sumant
Moolgaokar joined the Tata board, he remarked, 'At the
lunch table, you felt that Tata belonged to the nation.'

Dorab: This is an important part of Tata history. Jeh,
you have rattled off names of many exceptional business

leaders, and perhaps you, more than any of us, needed all of them in free, independent India. Sumant Moolgaokar in engineering, Faqir Chand Kohli in power and computers . . . how on earth did you attract them, and lead them?

Jeh: You know, early on I realized that I could not possibly manage all these businesses by myself. I realized that I was no genius. Further, my technical education was nipped in the bud because Dad asked me to join the business as early as 1924, when I was only twenty years old. So I went right out, looking for people who would be better than I was. I consciously gave them the space and visibility to stretch and deliver to their full potential. We had differences, but after some discussion and argument, I let them do things their way. In this regard I particularly recall A.D. Shroff, a hugely talented economist, but also given to strong opinions. I managed to get the best out of him for the nation and for Tata.

What would be the use of recruiting them and then subjugating them to my view, which had its own limitations?

Jamsetji: Well, well, I must say that it is a great tribute to you that you could do this. A true leader, I reckon, is one who is not so insecure that he needs to impose his views on others arising out of his status or position. True power must emanate from listening to others and from display of warmth. Authoritativeness and leadership emanate not necessarily from status but from these qualities. It sure is tough to be like that.

Saklatwala: Well, this has been a great conversation. All of us can feel happy that the institution which we all served and built continues to prosper. I pray that it continues to do so into the future too.

Jamsetji: I join you in your prayer. Like human beings, organizations too need renewal. Just one individual could have the power to renew an institution and ensure that it always meets the founding fathers' expectations, if he has two qualifications: first, he should have no past to hide, and second, he should have no personal expectations for the future.

10

Postscript

As we draw towards the end of this book we, the authors, are assailed with self-doubt with regard to some questions: what did we set out to do when we began the book? Have we fulfilled our goals? Why should the reader be interested in the contemporary relevance of Jamsetji Tata?

So far as we are concerned, we sought to uncover why Jamsetji is still relevant. We used the format of identifying the various Ps that defined Jamsetji's approach to entrepreneurship. We tried to illustrate each P through examples from three different periods since Jamsetji's times—the early period, the middle period and the recent period. We found that the greatness—and magic—of Jamsetji lay in the fact that all the Ps were adopted and executed at all times, almost synchronously, like an orchestra. Many great leaders and organizations have some of the Ps but while the Ps are individually necessary, they are not singly sufficient. In synchronization and harmony, the Ps seemed to produce exceptional results.

We reckon that questions on the relevance of Jamsetji these days can only be answered when the book is in the hands of the reader; the reader will need to judge the answers for themselves. We have tried our best to bring out the relevance of the great man, based on our deep and collective understanding of Tata, then and now.

Jamsetji's Lifetime

When Jamsetji was growing up, various parts of the Indian subcontinent were ruled by either the East India Company or by one of the several hundred maharajas of the princely states. During Jamsetji's lifetime, the world experienced Britain's Opium War in China, the entanglement of Britain in the Anglo-Afghan Wars, the dubious acquisition by England of the Kohinoor diamond from Maharaja Ranjit Singh's young son, the First War of Independence against the British by Indians, and the American Civil War accompanied by the much-acclaimed leadership of Abraham Lincoln. Jamsetji must have been influenced by all these events. He could well have read about how to usher in change in Abraham Lincoln's statement during the crisis of the American civil war, 'As our case is new, so we must think new, and act anew.'[1]

Jamsetji travelled incessantly across the world by boat and ship throughout his adult life. He must have learned about technology changes in the world, social transformations in communities and the making and unmaking of leaders in their quest for wealth and power. He would have noted the impressive results achieved by business start-ups initiated by industrialists like Thomas Alva Edison, Andrew Carnegie, Milton Hershey and William Hesketh Lever.

Throughout Jamsetji's life, he watched the rise of the new industrialists, as distinct from the earlier generation of businessmen-traders. He would have observed how they accumulated enormous wealth in their lifetime. He must have observed how the nature of enterprise drove their successful corporations to incessantly grow from big to bigger, and that size gave scale to the enterprise.

He must have become aware also of the derangement caused by economic power in some of those leaders in their quest for more and more. The most powerful men in the business world sometimes posed a conundrum to society. For example, in 1877, the founder of the Vanderbilt empire, Cornelius 'Commodore' Vanderbilt, told his son, 'Any fool can make a fortune; it takes a man of brains to hold it.' As Jamsetji grew older he might have become aware of how Cornelius's son, William Vanderbilt, felt about his father's wealth: 'Inherited wealth is a real handicap to happiness . . . it has left me with nothing to hope for, with nothing definite to seek or strive for.'[2]

One could validly say of Jamsetji that his defining characteristic was his combination of foresight and his ready acceptance, indeed his embracing, of change. This characteristic enabled Jamsetji to see the transformative impacts of change that others in his ecosystem could not: for example, that indigenous steel would be a very big thing for India, or that harnessing hydroelectric power could industrialize Bombay.

He must have observed that ownership and management were gradually getting separated because big enterprises could no longer be run by the founder or the founding family alone. While Jamsetji was still growing up, the richest man in the world was John Jacob Astor, who was worth $20 million when he died in 1848. He managed his successful enterprise with a handful of men and some clerks. But Jamsetji would have noted, from his incessant travels, that with the advent of railroads and steel, there was a need for the new concept of 'business manager'— and indeed such a profession was born in due course. Large enterprises needed to develop and nurture talented leaders because they could no longer run enterprises with a few men and personal hands-on oversight.

Jamsetji knew what he did not know; he accepted his deficiency of knowledge. That was why he hired people who knew more than he knew. He must have observed that the madhouses had many inmates with vision but that it was in the doing that wealth could be created. He needed those doers.

While it is possible that Jamsetji was aware of all the above-mentioned events and trends, the authors do not suggest that Jamsetji was in reality aware of all of those things. But he did know a lot of what was going on in the world— that is for sure. The past can be chronicled by historians, commented upon by contemporaries and analysed by posterity. What one can aver with certainty is that there is an intricate interconnection of facts, impressions, anecdotes, stories, history and influences lying buried in the past; also, that the past, the present and, arguably, the future too, are also invisibly interconnected, even though we may not be quite sure how and where those points of interconnection lie. Metaphorically, there is an ecosystem of events that have invisible and intricate connections, much like every tree and denizen of a forest is invisibly interconnected to every other in that ecosystem. Visionaries like Jamsetji develop an excellent grasp of this ecosystem.

After Jamsetji

Does much of what we have written in the book evidence the genius of Jamsetji? Yes, perhaps. But how did he institutionalize his values and genius? Did he do something to ensure that his successors felt aligned with his inalienable principles and were motivated to follow them while also changing what needed to be changed? It would appear that transformation and change were constant companions to his successors. After all, Jamsetji's enterprise began with the pursuit of textiles and steel, while his current successors are pursuing very different industry segments, such as semiconductors and digital platforms. This is a remarkable change, yet this is what the changing environment requires.

For sure, this dramatic change has happened over the course of a century and more, and it has been an evolutionary process. As the imaginary panel discussion in chapter 9 demonstrates, the group's businesses morphed continually—from textiles to steel, electricity and hospitality; from there to the newest and most relevant technologies, like truck-making, industrial chemicals and airlines; and further onwards from there to information processing, consumer goods, retailing electric vehicles and semiconductor chips!

It may sound dramatic to state it this way, but we wonder if Jamsetji and his successors represent for India what a combination of industrialists did for America: a sort of Andrew Carnegie (steel) plus Henry Ford (automotive) plus Conrad Hilton (hotels) plus Thomas J. Watson (information processing) plus Juan Trippe (airlines) plus

Sam Walton (retailing) plus Robert Noyce (microchips), all rolled into one.

Yet, through this transformational journey, the leadership of the group has always been aligned to one North Star—that the enterprise works for the benefit of the community. As J.R.D. Tata wrote in 1957 in his foreword to the biography *Jamsetji Nusserwanji Tata: A Chronicle of his Life*: 'Yet few men have played so vital a part in the renaissance of India and there is much to be learned even today from the life and work of this remarkable man.'[3]

He went on to say in the foreword:

> He lived his earlier part of life in one of the darkest periods in the long and chequered history of India. . . . He has an honoured place, for, as we look back upon his life, the part that he played in his own field was as important to India's rebirth as that of other great leaders. . . . he saw clearly that India's freedom could not be achieved or maintained by political means alone. . . . his policies continue to be followed . . . because his philosophy and his ideas on industrial management have been found to be sound and applicable even to the changed circumstances of the present day.

In his book, author and academic James O'Toole mentions that in the 1970s and 1980s, he had felt that a golden era had arrived and that enlightened capitalism was a new way of thinking about business and society.[4] By the 2000s, he found that only three of those many companies he had studied had maintained their admirable practices. The causes were change in leadership, ownership or their having gone bankrupt. He was disappointed with his forecast about the durability of enlightened capitalism.

He also found that a great many American business schools had retreated from including social responsibility, ethics and related subjects in their MBA curriculum. With disappointment, he averred that corporate virtue was difficult to maintain consistently. Further, corporate misconduct is forgiven quickly by investors, provided that the company recovers soon from its difficulties and restores high profit.[5]

Nearly all enlightened capitalists had attempted, in one form or another, to institutionalize their practices and to bake them into their organizational culture. James O'Toole found very few had succeeded.

If Jamsetji Tata has achieved some degree of success, what could be the overarching reasons for it? What are the lessons? Well, that is what this book is all about. In this age of terse and short communications, the authors would like to sign off with the key lessons for any enlightened business from the many preceding pages.

1. Adoption of a deep and abiding philosophy for the business early on. The four-point Vedantic recommendation is relevant here: first, self-awareness; second, protection of the resources (air, water, people) that enable one to conduct business; third, service to others before service to oneself; fourth, firm decision-making but with human compassion in implementation. Jamsetji Tata was, as mentioned earlier in this book, inspired by the philosophy of *Humata, Hukhta, Hvarshta*.

2. Celebration of the icons and their narratives through a rich tradition of rituals, oral history, archives and stories.
3. Maintaining the North Star through the inevitable turmoils that the business will encounter, determining what cannot and should not be transgressed. Admission of faults and correction if errors do occur.
4. Diligence and compassion in implementation of the hierarchy of the many stakeholders and beneficiaries.
5. Readiness to embrace the future at all times. The future is unknown and unclear. It is not an option to not embrace this ambiguous future if one wants to build longevity into the genes of the enterprise.

Acknowledgements

R. Gopalakrishnan

This is the first book that I have co-authored with Harish Bhat. Of the twenty books that I have written so far, this is the thirteenth that I have co-authored.

Co-authoring has helped me bring a broad perspective to writing, though it is harder work compared to writing alone. Co-authoring also has the additional benefit of encouraging others to share their wisdom and experiences through writing. This does not apply to Harish Bhat, who has been a successful author in his own right. I must acknowledge Harish for making it so rewarding to co-author with an experienced and bestselling author.

This is my sixth book with Penguin Random House, who, in fact, launched my first book in 2007. Milee Ashwarya has been a continuous source of support and encouragement through my journey. Hitha Haridas has painstakingly edited our manuscript for which I am grateful. PRH is a great publishing house to work with, and I would like to thank PRH.

I have had two employers, both very fine institutions: Hindustan Unilever and Tata. Whatever I have learnt and used as materials in this book has been born from experiences that I had in these two institutions. For this book, Tata companies and philosophies have been my main source of inspiration and instruction. I have been provoked to think deeply about how Tata has managed to top the charts of 'top business houses of India' for eighty-five years from 1939 till date. This is contrary to any statistic globally about the list of Fortune 500 companies. Amazing!

Lastly, for their patience with my doggedness, I must thank my family. As I concluded my first two careers—Hindustan Unilever and Tata—I decided to spend my 'third career' emptying myself of the experiential wealth acquired through half a century of life and company experiences. This has meant that concentrated work and travel have continued to take centre stage in my day. It is great to be able to do so, knowing that the family is doing whatever I am not doing.

Harish Bhat

I vividly recall how this book project came into my life. On 8 November 2022, I celebrated my sixtieth birthday. That same evening, I received a telephone call from R. Gopalakrishnan (RG).

'Harish, I have an idea for a book themed on Jamsetji Tata,' RG said, 'Would you like to be my co-author?'

Without hesitation, I said yes. I said yes because I admire and respect RG as a leader and as a writer. I said yes because RG has been my mentor on my writing voyage, ever since he helped me craft my first book twelve years ago. Co-authoring a book with one's guide is a dream come true.

I also said yes because Jamsetji Tata has been a huge source of inspiration for me throughout my working career, and writing this book would provide me a unique opportunity to take his ideas to the world at large.

That night, I told my wife, Veena, about this telephone call from RG, and she was equally delighted. This was, we agreed, the best sixtieth birthday gift that I could have received. My sincere thanks to R. Gopalakrishnan for having blessed me with this present. Thereafter, I have greatly enjoyed working with him as my co-author, and have learnt a lot from him during the writing of this book.

My sincere gratitude to the Tata Group, where I have been working for over thirty-seven years now, for having provided me such a wonderful professional home, and for having consistently encouraged me in my writing endeavours over the years. The group kindly provided me a sabbatical to write my first book, *Tata Log*, in 2012, and I have not looked back since then.

For the past eight years, during my tenure as brand custodian at the Tata Group, I have had the privilege of working under the leadership of N. Chandrasekaran, chairman, Tata Sons. I would like to thank him for constantly urging us to achieve world-class levels of excellence in everything we do. I have tried my best to be true to this aspiration, while writing this book.

Rajendra Prasad Narla, chief archivist at the Tata Central Archives, Pune, has been my constant partner in researching the history of the Tata Group. He has been most generous with his knowledge and time. He has also helped review the initial text of this book. I am grateful for his constant help and inputs.

I would like to acknowledge the many sources which I have referred to during the writing of this book. These are detailed in the bibliography.

To Milee Ashwarya and the team at Penguin Random House, thank you for your belief in my writing. Your encouragement and support have been invaluable in developing this book. Thank you, Milee, for the many conversations over the past several months, and for helping put structure to this somewhat complex project. Also, how can I forget that fabulous dinner conversation over sushi, sashimi and merlot at the Wasabi restaurant in the Taj, Mumbai, where many parts of this book came together beautifully in my mind?

Hitha Haridas, Saloni Mital and Kripa Raman have edited this book meticulously, and held this project together wonderfully well. Their editing prowess is complemented by their constant positivity and admirable professionalism. It has been a pleasure to work with all of you. Thank you for everything !

To my mother, Jayanthi, and my mother-in-law, Vatsala, I thank them for their blessings that provide me both support and reassurance. They are the elders of our family, and I look forward to gifting them the first two copies of this book. My mother rates each of my books objectively, on a scale of 1 to 10. I hope she gives this book a very good score.

My daughter, Gayatri, has been very encouraging of my writing efforts over the years. She is an avid reader, and I hope she enjoys reading this book. She is also a thoughtful critic, and I look forward eagerly to her views on what she loves about this book and what I could have done better.

My wife, Veena, has been my biggest source of encouragement and support throughout my writing journey. She stood by me staunchly when I took a sabbatical in 2012 to write my first book, which entailed stepping down from my role as COO of Titan. Many people told me then that this was a career limiting move, but Veena encouraged me to follow my passion and write, notwithstanding the potential risk to our family finances and my corporate career. In doing this, she gave me new wings to fly, for which I am ever grateful to her. With respect to this specific book, she constantly goaded me to keep up the momentum of writing. Whenever she saw any slackening on my part, she would talk to me about how best to put the project back on the rails. Her love and companionship have always provided me invaluable support.

I thank God Almighty for blessing me with the capability, passion and constant urge to write. Thanks to these divine blessings, I found my Ikigai as a writer. I hope and pray that I can put this wonderful gift to the best possible use throughout my life, by adding as much value as possible to every reader who chooses to read my books.

Notes

Chapter 1: Philosophy

1   Jamsetji Nusserwanji Tata: a chronicle of his life, FR Harris, Oxford University Press, 1925
2   *For the Love of India*, R.M. Lala.
3   *The Creation of Wealth*, R.M. Lala.
4   *The Tata Group*, Shashank Shah.
5   *Tatas: how a Family Built a Business and a Nation*, Girish Kuber.
6   *Story of Tata*, Peter Casey.
7   *Tata Log* and *Tata Stories*, Harish Bhat
8   TCS, L&T, Biocon, Marico, HDFC Group, Kotak Bank in the *Shapers of Business Institutions* series, Rupa, 2018-19.
9   *The Enlightened Capitalists*, James O'Toole, Harper Business, 2019.

Chapter 5: Progress: Making Choices for the Enterprise

1   *Men-Minutes-Money*, Thomas J. Watson, IBM, 1934.

2 *Building IBM*, Emerson W. Pugh, MIT Press,1995
3 Ibid.

Chapter 6: Persistence

1 *Giants of Enterprise*, Richard Tedlow, Harper Business, 2001.
2 *Giants of Enterprise*, Richard Tedlow, Harper Business, 2001
3 https://hbr.org/2012/10/12-guidelines-for-deciding-whe

Chapter 8: Profits

1 *Giants of Enterprise*, Richard S. Tedlow, Harper Business, 2001
2 *The Great Depression of 1990*, Ravi Batra, Simon & Schuster, 1987

Chapter 9: Perspectives

1 Published first in *Business Standard* on 29 July 2018

Chapter 10: Postscript

1 *Giants of Enterprise*, Richard Tedlow, Harper Business, 2001.
2 *Embrace the Future*, R. Gopalakrishnan and Hrishi Bhattacharyya, Bloomsbury, 2024.
3 *Jamsetji Nusserwanji Tata: a Chronicle of his Life*, Frank Harris, OUP, 1925.
4 *The Enlightened Capitalists*, James O'Toole, Harper, 2019.
5 *The Economist,* Schumpeter, 20 December 2014

Bibliography

Chapter 1: Philosophy

1. Tata Review, '60 years of nation building', October 2007.

Chapter 2: Purpose

1. Tata Review, 1997, vol. 32, December 2013.
2. https://youtu.be/68otfg601HI?feature=shared 'IN CONVERSATION WITH J. R. D. TATA'. Interview conducted by Rajiv Mehrotra, https://www.youtube.com/watch?v=68otfg601HI
3. *Good thoughts, Good Words, Good Deeds—A Book of Tata Quotes*, Tata Central Archives, 2019.
4. Ellekrog, Ole. *Guardian*, 9 January 2024.
5. Sandhu, Kiran D. *Roads to the Valley: The Legacy of Sardar Pritam Singh in Nepal*. India: Notion Press, 2023.
6. familybusinesscenter.com

Story 1. A Silk Farm for the Community

1. Lala, R. M. *For the Love of India: The Life and Time of Jamsetji Tata*, pp. 54–57. India: Penguin Random House India, 2004.
2. Harris, Frank. *Jamsetji Nusserwanji Tata: A Chronicle of his Life*, pp.103–107. India: Rupa Publications India, 2014.
3. Bhat, Harish. *#Tatastories: 40 Timeless Tales to Inspire You*, pp. 33–36. India: Penguin Random House India, 2021.
4. 'Fifty eventful years of service for the development of sericulture industry in Mysore state, Sri V.M. Appadhorai Mudaliar.' Brochure issued by Appadhorai's Sericultural Academy, Bangalore.

Story 2. Cancer Care for the Country

1. Lala, R. M. *The Heartbeat of a Trust*, pp. 69–79. India: McGraw-Hill Education, 1986.
2. Website of the Tata Trusts, tatatrusts.org, section on healthcare/cancer care.
3. Bhat, Harish. *#Tatastories: 40 Timeless Tales to Inspire You*, pp. 69–72. India: Penguin Random House India, 2021.

Story 3. Lakes, Trees and Trucks

1. Sharma, M. D. 'Mr. Moolgaokar, the Environmentalist', p. 29. *Telco Parivar*, August 1989.
2. Lala, R. M. *Beyond the Last Blue Mountain*, pp. 249–250. India: Penguin Random House India, 1992.
3. Tata Motors, 'The Power to Change Lives', April 2017, www.tatamotors.com.

Chapter 3: Pioneering

1. *Good Thoughts, Good Words, Good Deeds—A Book of Tata Quotes*, Tata Central Archives, 2019.

Story 1. Lighting up Lives

1. Harris, Frank. *Jamsetji Nusserwanji Tata: A Chronicle of His Life*, pp. 219–41. India: Rupa Publications India, 2014.
2. Lala, R. M. *For the Love of India: The Life and Times of Jamsetji Tata*, pp. 158–165. India: Penguin Random House India, 2004.
3. Bhat, Harish. *#Tatastories: 40 Timeless Tales to Inspire You*, pp. 37–40. India: Penguin Random House India, 2021.

Story 2. A Pilot Turns Pioneer: The Making of an Airline

1. Lala, R. M. *Beyond the Last Blue Mountain*, pp. 81–191. India: Penguin Random House India, 1992.
2. Kohli, M. S. 'Remembering JRD Tata'. In *JRD as Air Indians Remember*. India: Himalayan Books, 2010.
3. Dadabhoy, Bakhtiar K. *Jeh, A Life of J.R.D. Tata*, pp. 43–65. India: Rupa Publications India, 2005.

Story 3. Indica for India: The Nation's First Indigenous Car

1. Bhat, Harish. *Tatalog: Eight Modern Stories from a Timeless Institution*, pp. 20–49. India: Penguin Random House India, 2012.
2. Bhat, Harish. *#Tatastories: 40 Timeless Tales to Inspire You*, pp. 17–20. India: Penguin Random House India, 2021.

Chapter 4: People

1. JRD Tata's letter to K.C. Bhansali, 13 September 1965, Tata Central Archives.

Story 1. Talent for a Start-up: Jamsetji Tata and His Remarkable Leadership Team

1. Bio-data of Sir Bezonji Dadabhoy Mehta, Tata Central Archives.

2. Bio-data of Burjorji Padshah, Tata Central Archives.
3. Lala, R. M. *For the Love of India: The Life and Times of Jamsetji Tata*, pp. 174– 188. India: Penguin Random House India, 2004.
4. Keenan, John L. *A Steel Man in India*, pp. 37–38. New York: Duell, Sloan and Pearce, 1943.

Story 2. J.R.D. Tata: A Leader of Leaders

1. Lala, R. M. *Beyond the Last Blue Mountain*, pp. 244–254. India: Penguin Random House India, 1992.
2. Tata, J. R. D. *Letters*, edited by Arvind Mambro, p. 262. India: Rupa Publications India, 2004.
3. Kamath, M. V. *Nani A. Palkhivala: A Life*, pp. 95–98. India: Hay House India, 2007.

Chapter 5: Progress

1. J.R.D. Tata's interview in *Economic Times*, 17 September 1992.

Story 1. The Tata Shipping Line

1. Harris, Frank. *Jamsetji Nusserwanji Tata: A Chronicle of His Life*, pp. 91–98. India: Rupa Publications India, 2014.
2. Lala, R. M. *For the Love of India: The Life and Times of Jamsetji Tata*, pp. 76–84. India: Penguin Random House India, 2004.

Story 2. The Consistent and Disciplined Growth of TCS

1. Ramadorai, S. *The TCS Story . . . And Beyond*. India: Penguin Random House India, 2013.

Chapter 6: Persistence

Story 1. Creation of the IISc, Bangalore

1. Harris, Frank. *Jamsetji Nusserwanji Tata: A Chronicle of His Life*, pp. 113–145. India: Rupa Publications India, 2014.

2. Lala, R. M. *For the Love of India: The Life and Times of Jamsetji Tata*, pp. 105– 132. India: Penguin Random House India, 2004.
3. Letter from Jamsetji Tata to Swami Vivekananda, 23 November 1898, Tata Central Archives.
4. Basu, Sankari Prasad Basu. 'Vivekananda, Nivedita and Tata's Research Scheme'. *Prabuddha Bharata*, 1978.

Story 2. Tata Chemicals and Darbari Seth

1. Chacko, Philip and Christabelle Noronha. *Salt of the Earth: The Story of Tata Chemicals*, pp. 29–90. India: Westland Books India, 2014.
2. Lala, R. M. *The Creation of Wealth*, pp. 85–90. India: Penguin Random House India, 1981.
3. Lala, R. M. *Beyond the Last Blue Mountain*, pp. 251–54. India: Penguin Random House India, 1992.

Story 3. Belief and Resilience: The Early Years of Tanishq

1. Bhat, Harish. *Tatalog: Eight Modern Stories from a Timeless Institution*, pp. 82– 104. India: Penguin Random House India, 2012.
2. Kamath, Vinay. *Titan: Inside India's Most Successful Consumer Brand*, pp. 99–124. India: Hachette India, 2018.

Chapter 7: Principles

1. Burlingham, Bo. *Small Giants: Companies that Choose to Be Great Instead of Big*. Australia: Penguin Books Australia, 2007.

Story 1. Saving Tata Steel

1. Keenan, John L. *A Steel Man in India*, pp. 72–91. New York: Duell, Sloan and Pearce, 1943.
2. Nath, Aman and Jay Vithalani. *Horizons: The Tata-India Century, 1904–2004*, pp. 87, 103, 111. India: India Book House, 2004.

3. Lala, R. M. *The Creation of Wealth*, pp. 27–29. India: Penguin Random House India, 1981.
4. Bhat, Harish. *#Tatastories: 40 Timeless Tales to Inspire You*, pp. 46–50. India: Penguin Random House India, 2021.

Story 2. The Dilemmas of J.R.D. Tata

1. Lala, R. M. *Beyond the Last Blue Mountain*, pp. 105–106. India: Penguin Random House India, 1992.
2. Lala, R. M. 'The Business Ethics of J.R.D. Tata'. *CIB Espirit* Vol. 1, Issue 3, 2014.
3. Irani, J. J. *Doctor Steel: My Life and Times*, pp 33–34. India: Penguin Random House India, 2023.

Story 3. Tata Finance Runs into Trouble

1. Bhat, Harish. *Tatalog: Eight Modern Stories from a Timeless Institution*, pp. 69–81. India: Penguin Random House, 2012.
2. 'Grime and Salvation'. *Tata Review*, Vol. No. XXXIX, Issue 4, October–December 2004.

Chapter 8: Profits

1. Jackson, Ira and Jane Nelson. *Profit with Principles: Seven Strategies for Delivering Value with Values*. Broadway Books, 2004.

Story 1. The Story of Empress Mills

1. Harris, Frank. *Jamsetji Nusserwanji Tata: A Chronicle of His Life*, pp. 23–46, 107–112. India: Rupa Publications India, 2014.
2. Bhat, Harish. *#Tatastories: 40 Timeless Tales to Inspire You*, pp. 29–32. India: Penguin Random House India, 2021.
3. Speech delivered by Jamsetji Tata, 5 April 1895, Tata Central Archives.

4.   Central India Spinning, Weaving and Manufacturing Company Limited. Annual Reports, Vol. 1, 1875–1932.

Story 2. A Truly Good Cup of Coffee

1.   Tata Coffee Ltd. Annual Reports, 2021–22, 2022–23.
2.   Nambisan Kaveri. *Cherry Red, Cherry Black: The Story of Coffee in India*. India: Bloomsbury Publishing India Pvt Ltd, 2022.

Story 3. The Fight against COVID-19

1.   'Inside the Tata Response to Covid-19', Tata.com.

Scan QR code to access the
Penguin Random House India website